5 2B.

PERSPECTIVES ON ECONOMIC THOUGHT

THE AUTHOR

Born in 1941, Giovanni Palmerio studied at the Universities of Bologna and Cambridge. He taught at the Universities of Ancona, Venice and Naples. Since 1976 he has been Full Professor of Economics at the Libera Università Internazionale degli Studi Sociali (LUISS) of Rome, where he is also Head of the Department of Economic Studies. He was Chancellor of the University of Molise. He has been economic adviser to the Ministry of Labour, the Ministry of the Budget and the Ministry of the "Mezzogiorno". Since 1990 he has been the President of the National Institute for Economic Forecasts (ISCO). He is the Director of the journal "Economia, Società e Istituzioni" and a member of the scientific committee of various journals. He is the author of many books and articles on cycles, growth and development theory, public finance and inflation.

PERSPECTIVES ON ECONOMIC THOUGHT

Giovanni Palmerio
Department of Economics,
LUISS University, Rome

DARTMOUTH

Aldershot · Brookfield USA · Hong Kong · Singapore · Sydney

Published by
Dartmouth Publishing Company
Gower House
Croft Road
Aldershot
Hants GU11 3HR

Dartmouth Publishing Company
Old Post Road
Brookfield
Vermont 05036
USA

British Library Cataloguing in Publication Data
Palmerio, Giovanni, 1941-
Perspectives on economic thought.
1. Economic thought. Perspectives
I. Title

ISBN 1 85521 189 0

Laserset by Computype Manuscript Services, Standard House, 49 Lawrence Street, York

Printed in Great Britain by Billing & Sons Ltd, Worcester

Contents

Foreword

It is always flattering to be asked to write the foreword to a distinguished and important book. It is even more of a pleasure when the author is like Giovanni Palmerio, an old and trusted friend. Giovanni Palmerio is at the centre of the Italian Policy Community. He is currently Director of the Institute of Economic Studies at LUISS, the independent University of the Social Sciences in Rome. He previously held academic appointments at Ancona, Venice and Naples. In recent years he has been instrumental in establishing the Campobasso campus of the University of Molise, of which he was acting Vice-Chancellor for a time. However, Giovanni Palmerio is anything but an ivory-towered academic. For some years he was Mayor of his home town of Guardiagrele. Within his native province, Abruzzo, he has been very active and currently heads the Regional Economics Research Institute (IARES) at Chieti. However, most of his policy advice has been dispensed at the central level. In recent years, he has been the Chief Economic Adviser to the Agenzia per il Mezzogiorno, the institution responsible for the Italian government's massive programme to revitalise the southern economy. In November 1990, he became President of ISCO, the Italian Forecasting Institute with a remit roughly similar to that of the Congressional Budget Office. Thus, Giovanni Palmerio is a man of many parts who has been in the thick of Italian policy-making at all levels.

I read a previous edition of the present book in Italian several years ago. I found it a most stimulating, indeed exciting, experience. It seems

ix

to me that there are two broad traditions in economics. One is the Anglo-Saxon neoclassical tradition with which we are all familiar. The other may loosely be termed the Continental tradition of which the Austrian and Marxian are the two best known but by no means the only strands. The importance of Giovanni Palmerio's book lies in the fact that it is an extremely accessible presentation of economics from the Continental view. The first thing that will strike the reader is that it contains no diagrams – this in a book which in Italy has been used as a textbook. In itself this illustrates the difference between the two approaches referred to above. There is a strong argument for saying that a copy of this book should be lodged in every library for the benefit of prospective economics teachers in schools and colleges. They would all gain from realising that where appropriate, *any* topic in economics can be explained without a single diagram especially in these days of ever more diverse students. However, the main value of this book lies in its comprehensive nature. Virtually all aspects of economics and economic policy are dealt with at some point in the book. This reflects an important feature of the Continental approach. Anglo-Saxon economists tends to compartmentalise the subject, whereas Continental economists believe that it is impossible to analyse any one aspect of the subject without considering the inter-relationship with all others. Hence, Giovanni has written an extremely lucid, coherent account of economics and economic problems from a Continental perspective. I think that this is both a unique and a useful contribution to the subject.

David Gowland
University of York

1 Neoclassical microeconomics

1.1 CONSUMER BEHAVIOUR

At the beginning of the Thirties economics was dominated by the *neoclassical* or *marginalistic approach*, founded around 1870 by Jevons (from Britain), Menger (from Austria) and Walras (from France). Neoclassical economics has a predominantly microeconomic character, in that it studies the behaviour of single economic units, or, rather, of individuals – consumers, entrepreneurs, etc. – facing different situations. The neoclassical approach contains only a few macroeconomic elements, i.e. concepts referring to the whole economy, such as a country's total production, overall consumption and investment.

The study of the behaviour of consumers and of firms is particularly important for microeconomic analysis. Consumer theory considers an individual with a given income and addresses the question of how his income is spent. What goods are bought and in what quantity? The consumer attempts to maximise the *utility* or pleasure or satisfaction he derives from consuming goods. The quantity of goods he buys depends on his *tastes*, the available *income* and the *price*s of the goods. When the individual purchases the quantities of goods that guarantee the maximum attainable utility, given personal tastes, income and the price of goods, a position termed *equilibrium* is attained. This position is called equilibrium because the subject has no wish to leave it, that is, to change

1

the quantities of goods consumed, for instance to consume more meat and less fish, since this would reduce his satisfaction. The individual changes his equilibrium choices only if there is a change in his tastes, income or in the prices of goods. When this happens a new position of equilibrium occurs.

Microeconomic consumption theory also analyses the movement from one equilibrium position to another. In general, if an individual's tastes change but his income and the prices of goods remain unchanged, the individual purchases more of those goods that give him a greater satisfaction.

An increase in an individual's income, with tastes and the prices of goods remaining the same, leads to a higher consumption of all goods. The exception to this rule is 'inferior' goods, for example, potatoes or bread. An individual with a very low income buys a large quantity of bread or potatoes because he cannot buy highly priced foodstuffs such as meat, fish and cheese. As his income increases, he purchases more of these goods and less bread and fewer potatoes. Finally, if the price of a good falls, other things remaining equal, the consumer purchases a higher quantity of it. Again, however, this rule has an exception in the case of inferior goods. Consider, for example, an individual with a monthly income of £500 who purchases just two commodities, potatoes and meat, and that the price of potatoes is 25 p per lb, and the price of meat is £2 per lb. Assume that, given the individual's preferences, maximum utility is reached when 400 lbs of potatoes and 200 lbs of meat are bought (in this way, the individual spends all his income: 0.25 x 400 + 2 x 200). Then the price of potatoes goes down to 20 p per lb. If the individual in question were to continue buying 400 lbs of potatoes, he would spend £80 instead of £100 and would have £20 left which could be spent on meat. However, the individual might decide, on the basis of his preferences, to consume less than 400 lbs of potatoes, in order to raise his consumption of meat. However, these are exceptional cases, since an individual normally consumes more of a commodity when its price goes down and vice versa.

1.2 FIRMS' BEHAVIOUR

The behaviour of firms is analysed by criteria similar to those adopted for consumer theory. From a combination of different factors of production (plant, machinery, raw materials, labour), the firm produces a commodity. It obtains a revenue from the sale of this commodity, but must incur production costs. The difference between revenue and costs represents profits. The firm produces the quantity that ensures maximum profits.

As the amount produced and sold increases, so do the firm's revenues and costs, although usually not at the same rate. The level of production (that is, the quantity of goods produced) giving a firm the maximum profit varies according to the rate of increase respectively of revenue and costs. This level of production represents the firm's equilibrium position. It changes, that is the quantity produced increases or falls, only when there is a change in the demand for the commodity by consumers or when there is a change in the production costs of the commodity itself.

1.3 THE DERIVATION OF SUPPLY AND DEMAND

Consumer theory maintains that, except in the case of inferior goods, an individual (with unchanged tastes and income) purchases a larger quantity of a commodity when its price drops. In economic terms, this means that an agent reduces his/her demand for a commodity when its price increases and increases demand when the price falls. This rule applies to all agents.

Let us consider a number of individuals who wish to purchase commodities (for example, bread, meat or television sets). If the price of a commodity is high, many individuals (except those with a very high income) demand a limited quantity of it, while most consumers are unable to buy it. As the price of the commodity falls, more people buy it, and in greater quantities. Thus, the total demand for a commodity, i.e. the *collective* or *market demand*, which is equal to the sum of individuals' demands, gradually increases as the price of the commodity falls, or diminishes when the price of the commodity rises.

Moreover, for each commodity there are, apart from individuals wishing to buy it, many firms wanting to sell (i.e. to supply) it. The supply of a commodity normally goes up when its price increases.

In fact, when the price of a commodity increases, firms are more willing to produce it and try to sell it in greater quantities, because this allows them to raise their profits. Suppose, for instance (and this is a normal hypothesis), that the marginal cost of producing a commodity (that is, the cost of producing an additional unit of the commodity) rises gradually as the firm expands production. In this case, the higher the price of the commodity, the more the firm can expand production. In other words, the maximum profit (that is the firm's equilibrium position) corresponds to a higher production level the higher the price of the commodity.

Moreover, when the price of a commodity increases, even the least efficient firms (i.e. the firms which have higher production costs) are able to sell it. Thus the total supply of a commodity (called *collective* or *market supply*) increases as its price rises.

1.4 MARKET EQUILIBRIUM

Suppose now that the price of a commodity, for instance meat, is very high, so that the supply of meat is high while the demand is low. Some of the meat remains unsold and the producers are forced to reduce the price. In this way, demand increases and supply drops until they become equal. The price that equates the quantity of meat demanded to that supplied is termed *equilibrium price*.

An important conclusion can now be drawn: the equilibrium price of a commodity is determined by the market demand for and the market supply of the commodity itself.

As we have seen, market demand is the sum of demands from individuals. In turn, demand for a commodity from an individual also depends on the individual's tastes, i.e. on the structure of his preferences. *The market clearing price for a commodity is therefore determined by the tastes of individuals.* We shall see in due course that this conclusion, representing the foundation of neoclassical or marginalistic theory, is one of the most controversial points in modern theories on price determination, some of which reject the neoclassical approach and go back to the classical school (whose main representatives were Adam Smith in the Eighteenth century and Ricardo and Marx in the Nineteenth).

1.5 GENERAL EQUILIBRIUM

The study of a single consumer or firm is described as *partial equilibrium analysis*. This kind of analysis also occurs when the price determination of a commodity is examined as a result of the supply and demand for the commodity itself.

Several neoclassical economists had a more ambitious aim: they did not study price formation for a single commodity but the process of price formation for all commodities at the same time. This is the problem of *general equilibrium*, analysed for the first time in 1874 by the French economist Walras, taken up by Pareto (from Italy) and reconsidered in the 1930s by a number of German and Scandinavian economists such as Neisser, von Stackelberg, Zeuthen and the mathematicians von Neumann (from Austria) and Wald (from Hungary).

The demand for a commodity, such as sugar, depends not only on the price of that commodity, but also on the price of many others. If the price of tea (which is a *complementary commodity* to sugar) were to go down, the demand for tea and thus for sugar would increase. If the price of saccharin, which is a substitute for sugar, were to go down, the demand for saccharin would increase and that for sugar would decrease.

A similar phenomenon occurs for supply. There are goods *joint in supply*: for example, sheep give both meat and wool. If the price of wool increases, it is profitable to expand flocks to increase wool production, but then meat production also rises. Consequently, meat supply depends not only on the price of meat but also on that of wool.

From these examples it can be inferred that the demand for each commodity depends upon the price of different goods, and the same conclusion can be drawn concerning supply. General equilibrium theory analyses the process through which all prices are determined simultaneously and equate each commodity's supply and demand.

General equilibrium theory starts from the analysis of the behaviour of consumers and firms and considers the process whereby all consumers try to maximise utility and all firms try to maximise profits. This behaviour determines the supply and demand for each commodity and thus the prices that equate the supply and demand for each.

The price of goods, as already mentioned, is determined by supply and demand. The (collective) demand for each commodity is determined by the sum of individuals' demands for that commodity. These, in turn, are determined by individuals' tastes. *Thus, in general equilibrium theory the basic conclusion of neoclassical analysis still applies in that prices of goods are also determined by the preferences of individuals.*

1.6 MARKET STRUCTURE, THE THEORY OF PERFECT COMPETITION AND ITS CRISIS

Even if one accepts the hypothesis that a firm always aims at maximising its profits, its behaviour differs according to the context in which it operates. For example, a firm that is the sole producer of a certain commodity (a *monopoly* situation) can influence its price. On the other hand, a firm cannot influence the prices of the goods it produces if these goods are produced by many firms (a *competitive* situation). In this case, the firm that raised its price would lose all its customers. In a monopoly, however, whoever needs a particular commodity is forced to purchase it from the sole producer at the price fixed by the latter. Thus, firms behave in a different way according to the context in which they operate, that is, according to the market structure.

Up to the end of the Twenties, economists had only analysed two basic market structures: pure (or perfect) competition and pure monopoly. However, they tended to concentrate on the first. General equilibrium theory, moreover, was based exclusively on the hypothesis that firms operate in a purely competitive environment.

The main features of this market structure are the *homogeneity of product* and the *atomisation of the market*.

The first assumption implies that every commodity has unique characteristics and that no other good may substitute it perfectly. Obviously there are different commodities or different types of the same commodity like, for example, durum wheat and common wheat, each of which produces a different type of bread. But there are no different commodities with an identical function: this concept is expressed in

6

technical terms by affirming that there is no product differentiation. For example, the soap-powder market is not a purely competitive market because different products perform the same function but are presented in a different way, given that each firm claims that its product is of a higher quality than the others. Thus, one firm produces Brand X, another one Brand Y and so on, while in pure competition there are countless firms that produce durum wheat on the one hand and countless firms that produce common wheat on the other.

The second characteristic, the atomised market, implies that each commodity is produced by a very large number of firms, all of a limited size, and that none can influence its price. Also excluded is the possibility that some firms might agree among themselves in order to raise the price; were they to do so, they would lose all their purchasers.

Thus there is the real possibility that a new firm could enter the market. Since firms are all small, neither large amounts of capital nor specialised technical knowledge are necessary to enter the industry.

For this situation to remain unchanged over time, firms must remain small, that is, they must not expand. According to the theory of pure competition, the expansion of production does not take place through the growth of existing firms, but rather through the creation of new ones.

In practice, however, even at the end of the last century it became clear that this was not so. Moreover, during the century many industries expanded not so much because new firms entered the industry, but as a result of the growth of those firms that already existed, for example in the automobile industry.

The British economist Alfred Marshall had already noticed this phenomenon at the end of the last century. He attributed it above all to the existence of *internal economies*, that is, to the opportunity that a firm has, when expanding production, of reducing its average costs (total costs divided by the number of units produced), thereby achieving a more efficient organisation and a greater division of labour. It can also introduce technologically more advanced machinery. These are all things that a small firm finds more difficult to do.

Marshall tried to reconcile the reality with pure competition theory, through a series of logical progressions, but with little success. In 1925 the Italian economist Piero Sraffa showed that Marshall's attempt to reconcile the enlargement of firms with pure competition was not possible and, given that the growth in size of firms was by then an important and

7

generalised phenomenon, he advised scholars to start analysing monopoly rather than pure competition.

1.7 MONOPOLY, IMPERFECT COMPETITION AND OLIGOPOLY

Firms increase their size to a large extent through a process of concentration, so that the number of firms contracts. When a commodity is produced by only a few firms (as happens today in many industries), these agree among themselves to alter the price of the goods they produce. Thus a situation is created that is no longer competitive but is similar to that of monopoly.

Pure monopoly had already been studied at the beginning of the Nineteenth century by the French economist Augustin Cournot. However, pure monopoly, by assuming that a firm is the sole producer of a particular commodity, is not realistic in itself. In practice, market structures are intermediate between pure competition and monopoly: they can be classified as *imperfect* (or *monopolistic*) *competition* and *oligopoly*.

Imperfect or *monopolistic competition* was analysed from the Thirties on by economists in Europe and the United States such as Joan Robinson, Chamberlin, von Stackelberg, Amoroso and Vinci. These authors focus on a market structure which is closer to pure competition than to monopoly, because it is characterised by a large number of firms. However, products are not homogeneous as in perfect competition, but *differentiated*. A typical example of monopolistic competition is the soap-powder market, which was discussed earlier. There are various brands of soap-powder, each produced by a different firm, and many people are prepared to pay a slightly higher price for a particular soap-powder which they consider to be of a better quality than another. The firm therefore has a certain influence on the price of the goods it produces.

A still greater influence on the price of the commodity is that of a firm operating in an *oligopoly*. The latter is a market structure where the production of a commodity is concentrated in the hands of a few firms. A typical example is the automobile industry in Italy or France, where production is dominated by three or four large companies, each of which can influence the price of its product.

In an oligopoly there are a few firms that can agree to fix a price,

8

creating a situation similar to a monopoly; alternatively they attempt to compete among each other, in which case each firm tries to attract customers from its rivals. A firm that wishes to exclude rivals from the market has to implement a strategy, consisting of tactics such as lowering the price of its product, improving its quality, advertising widely and so on. The British economist Rothschild was especially concerned with these possibilities, whilst von Neumann and Morgenstern (Austrians, one a mathematician and the other an economist who both subsequently moved to the United States) devised mathematical *Game Theory* which can be used to explain the behaviour of oligopolistic firms. The results obtained in this way, however, are usually far removed from reality.

Other authors, such as Bain and Sylos Labini, have maintained that oligopolistic firms generally reach an agreement and fix a price for the goods they produce. This price will be high enough to guarantee a large profit margin. However, this must not be too great, or other firms, attracted by the presence of high profits, enter the market and begin to produce these goods.

Nevertheless, other firms cannot always get into the industry because the production of goods offered in an oligopolistic market frequently requires considerable financial resources and technical expertise. For example, it is not easy for just anyone to start producing washing machines, although a large firm that already produces refrigerators should be able to do so without great difficulty.

Unlike the theory of pure competition, oligopoly theory does not provide a unique solution to the problem of price determination. This is one of the reasons why the analysis of oligopoly has remained almost exclusively within the field of partial equilibrium, while the theory of general equilibrium is generally based on the hypothesis that firms operate in a competitive environment.

1.8 MONOPOLY, PUBLIC INTERVENTION, INDUSTRIAL COALITIONS, MONOPSONY AND OLIGOPSONY, BILATERAL MONOPOLY

A firm operating in monopoly or oligopoly conditions can influence the price of the goods it sells by increasing it, which is something that a firm operating in perfect competition cannot do. From this it has been inferred that *the existence of monopolies has a negative effect on consumers and thus on society*, whilst free competition achieves the maximum welfare for society.

In many sectors technological progress and mass production have brought about the disappearance of small firms and the concentration of production in the hands of a few large firms (sometimes even only in one). Modern methods of production often require extensive plant and technologically advanced machinery, that can only be acquired by large companies. Thus, a *process of technical and financial concentration* (i.e. of capital) has occurred. This has brought about the formation of large monopolistic firms in a large number of industries. Concentration has its good points, given that it leads to a reduction of the costs of production. A large monopolistic firm can produce at much lower costs than a small competitive one, because it can exploit human and technological resources to the full, by buying advanced machinery that produces large quantities of goods. Consequently, the problem facing modern economies is that of letting large firms exist and benefiting from the advantages derived from a reduction of costs and technological innovation, whilst simultaneously preventing them from exploiting the monopoly situation that they enjoy to the detriment of consumers. The state, in other words, should control the prices of monopolistic firms, by preventing them from fixing prices at too high a level. The main industrial countries, in particular the United States, have enacted *antitrust laws* for this purpose.

In several countries, such as France, Italy and the United Kingdom, the state, as well as adopting an antitrust policy, has nationalised some firms that were previously privately owned. The *nationalisation* of a private firm means that the ownership and the management of the firm is transferred to the state. Some private firms which have been nationalised operated previously as monopolies and have thus become *public monopolies*. The postal service, the railways and so on are examples of public monopolies. When a public monopoly is run correctly, it should have all the advantages of size, together with low prices, but in practice this is not always the case. In the Eighties the British Government introduced a policy of 'privatisation', or denationalisation, of many state owned companies selling part of, or all, their shares to private individuals. Many of the companies privatised have come from a number of sectors that were traditionally state monopolies, such as telecommunications and transport, and energy, for example British Telecom (1984), British Gas

10

(1986), British Airways (1987), Rolls Royce (1987), the British Airports Authority (1987), British Steel (1988), Water Authorities (1989) and the electric industry (1990).

The aim was to increase efficiency and improve the quality of goods and services. In fact, the privatised industries in the United Kingdom have recently shown a tendency to produce greater profits.

1.8.1 Industrial coalitions

When several large firms agree to undertake a common market policy, they form a *coalition*. Normally this agreement does not aim to prevent other firms (usually small ones) from operating in the market, nor to shut out foreign competitors. The common policy may relate to setting the price, the quantity of goods that each firm should produce, or the geographical division of sales among the firms participating in the agreement: in practice it aims to control the market. In this way, the firms hope to avoid unnecessary in-fighting. These agreements, called *industrial coalitions*, take the form of *cartels* or *trusts*. In the first case, originating in Germany, each firm remains autonomous; in the second one, which applies to the United States, firms come under one management. Trusts often lead to mergers among firms, which become organisations under a single management. From the point of view of technological innovation and of the reduction of costs, coalitions have the advantages of a concentration. Antimonopolistic laws have been introduced in relation to such groups; these laws seek to retain the advantages of the arrangements but also to prevent industrial coalitions from exercising a monopoly power in price fixing and market control.

1.8.2 Monopsony and oligopsony, bilateral monopoly

In all the examples given until now, monopoly and oligopoly relate to supply, in the sense that we have always considered one or a limited number of producers, but many consumers. However, there are also cases of monopoly and oligopoly on the demand side, called respectively monopsony and oligopsony. *Monopsony* occurs when a commodity is produced by many firms, but there is only one consumer for it. *Oligopsony* occurs when a commodity is produced by many firms, but only a few consumers demand it.

11

In the case of monopsony, the single consumer (or *monopsonist*) imposes the price of the good on the producers. The monopsonist tries to impose a very low price. This price, however, cannot be lower than the production costs of the commodity, otherwise firms would not be able to produce the goods and would go bankrupt. Suppose, for example, that certain agricultural enterprises produce oranges. These enterprises are small and located far away from the final market, so that they sell their oranges to a single wholesaler, who collects them and then sells them on. If the wholesaler is the only purchaser because there is nobody else in the area to do so, the wholesaler is able to fix the price at which he is prepared to purchase the oranges. In oligopsony, the stronger the agreement among the purchasers (called *oligopsonists*), the lower the selling price that they impose on producers.

Finally, it may be that monopoly (or oligopoly) conditions prevail on both the supply and demand side of the market; this is what is called a *bilateral monopoly. Labour market* conditions often resemble a bilateral monopoly. In practice, both workers (who supply labour) and entrepreneurs (who demand labour) are organised by their respective associations which negotiate on labour costs, i.e. wages. The workers have their trade union, that is the sole seller of labour, while industrialists have their own association, that is the only purchaser of labour. In this case wages are high or low depending upon whether the trade union has a bigger political and contractual power than the industrialists association, or vice versa. For example, if the trade union has the power to organise strikes, to influence the public opinion in favour of workers, and to induce workers to work harder, then the industrialists association may have to concede large wage increases.

2 Keynes

2.1 MACROECONOMICS AND NATIONAL ACCOUNTING

The British economist John Maynard Keynes (1883-1946) represents an important turning-point in economics. One of the main innovations he introduced consists of focusing not so much on the behaviour of individual economic units, that is the firm and the consumer, but on the aggregate quantities of the economy, such as total consumption, total investment and total production. When the behaviour of individual economic units is analysed, this is called *microeconomics*. When the quantities relating to the economy as a whole or to its individual sectors are considered, this is *macroeconomics*; total quantities are called macroeconomic or aggregate quantities.

The fundamental concept of Keynesian analysis is *gross national product* (GNP) or *gross national income*. GNP represents the sum of all final goods and services produced in a country during a given period, usually a year. For example, in 1990 Britain's GNP is represented by all the final goods and services produced from 1 January to 31 December. These include goods such as bread, meat, refrigerators, and services, for instance medical visits, a teacher's lecture, a haircut. Since these are heterogeneous quantities, they can only be summed as follows: the amounts of goods and services produced are to be each multiplied by their respective price and then added up.

In calculating GNP, however, only *final* goods and services should be considered. This point can be illustrated by the following example: suppose that in a year a given quantity of wool is produced, which is spun and then transformed into cloth and then again transformed into dresses. Only the dresses should be included in the calculation of GNP, because they are the final goods, while wool and cloth are intermediate goods. If they were included in GNP, there would clearly be some double counting.

Gross National Income is given by the sum of all incomes (wages, profits, interests and rents) received by individuals in a year. It is always equal to GNP. In modern economies, where incomes are calculated in monetary terms, this may not be immediately apparent; however, it may be easily grasped when we think of it in physical terms. Consider a barter economy where a firm produces a certain commodity, such as dresses. The firm uses the dresses it produces in the following way: it gives part of them as a payment for those firms providing the intermediate goods necessary to produce the dresses, such as material, buttons,etc. .The remaining dresses are used to pay for other expenses (for example, the rent of the premises, interests, etc.) and to pay workers (wages). The dresses eventually left over represent the firm's profits.

Production (income produced) is thus distributed among the different agents that take part in production. The sum of the goods produced is equal to the sum of individuals' incomes: this relationship, or rather the identity between GNP and Gross National Income, is such that the two terms are interchangeable. In the example above, each agent receives a payment in kind (dresses) but, since by assumption we are dealing with a barter economy, he can purchase other goods with this income.

Gross National Income, again, is the sum of all incomes received by economic agents in a year: incomes from dependent labour (wages and salaries); incomes from autonomous (non-dependent) labour such as, for example, those of traders and professional men; firms' earnings (profits); interests; rents; etc. .

Economic agents (firms, workers) give part of their income to the state[1] by paying taxes. According to accounting procedures, the incomes of economic agents are usually calculated gross of direct taxes (namely, they include them), but not of indirect ones. Consequently, Gross National Income is given by the sum of the incomes listed above plus indirect taxes.

The state however gives back part of the income it receives through taxes to other subjects in the form of pensions, unemployment benefits and other subsidies. These incomes do not represent the remuneration for an activity that has been carried out; rather, they are *transfers* (of revenue) made by the state from certain citizens (that pay taxes) to others (pensioners, unemployed, etc.). These transfers are not included in the calculations of Gross National Income. If, for example, pensions were to be included in national income, an income that has already been considered as the income of people paying taxes would be counted twice.

The goods and services which are produced can be put to one of the following uses: consumption, investment, or exportation. Consequently, GNP, which is the sum of all final goods and services, is equal to the sum of consumption (both private and public) plus investment (private and public) plus exports. Since all goods and services have one of these uses, the sum of these three components is equal to total production.

Examples of consumer goods include foodstuffs, clothes, cars, household appliances. The last three are consumer durable goods. Public consumption consists of goods and services that the state supplies to its citizens: education, defence, justice, the health service, etc. .

Investment includes construction (houses, bridges, roads), plant and machinery, etc. . Investment is classified as private or public according to whether it is made by firms or by the state.[2] Finally, exports are goods produced domestically and sold abroad; therefore they are included in GNP. They may be both consumer goods and investment goods.

2.2 THE PRE-KEYNESIAN THEORY OF EMPLOYMENT

In a primitive economy goods are distributed in kind to the citizens who have taken part in production. On the contrary, things are different in a modern economy. In fact, the goods that are produced are brought to the market, where the agents see them and wish to buy them. As we saw in chapter one, there is a demand and supply for each commodity. In macroeconomics, the concepts of *total* (or *aggregate*) *demand* and *total* (or *aggregate*) *supply* represent respectively the demand and supply not of a single commodity but of all the goods and services existing in the economy.

The point may be made clear if one considers that GNP, which is the sum of all goods and services produced, is defined as a single output. Then it may be imagined that a demand and supply relative to this output actually exists. What happens if total demand is greater than total supply?

We know from microeconomics that, when the demand for a commodity is greater than its supply, its price goes up. This causes the quantity demanded to fall and the quantity supplied to rise. The process goes on until the price reaches its equilibrium value, making the two quantities equal.

The analysis can be easily transposed in macroeconomic terms: when total demand is greater than total supply, the prices of goods go up. This causes a drop in demand and an expansion in supply, until an equilibrium price is reached, where total demand and total supply are equal. When demand is lower than supply, the opposite takes place.

For each commodity price flexibility ensures that demand and supply become the same, i.e. it brings all markets to equilibrium, and thus ensures equality between total demand and total supply. Such a situation is called *macroeconomic equilibrium*; the quantities of (final) goods and services produced in such an equilibrium represent the *equilibrium* or *actual national income*, i.e. the *national income actually produced*. On the other hand, the production level (that is the quantity of goods and services) achieved in a country when all the existing resources (i.e. all workers and all plant and machinery) are fully employed takes the name of *potential* (or *full employment*) *national income*.

The obvious question that arises is whether the level of equilibrium income, i.e. of income actually produced, is always equal to potential income.

At first sight, nothing assures equality. In fact, it could happen that markets have prices that equalize the demand and supply for goods, but at the same time there is unemployment and capital (plant and machinery) laying idle. In this situation the quantities of goods produced are not the maximum quantities that may be obtained, i.e. effective income is lower than the potential one. This situation represents an *underemployment equilibrium*: it is an equilibrium because total demand and total supply are equal, but nevertheless workers are unemployed and machinery is idle (which explains the term 'underemployment').

On the other hand most pre-Keynesian economists maintained that equilibrium income was always equal to potential income, thanks to a mechanism that worked essentially through the labour market. Here there are firms looking for workers, that is, demanding labour, and there are workers supplying their services. The wage level represents the price of labour; it is determined by the demand and supply of labour, according to the same mechanism of microeconomic analysis that applies to all goods. For example, if the equilibrium income is lower than the potential one, there are unemployed workers. This means that labour supply exceeds the firms' demand for workers' services. Thus wages fall and this leads firms to hire more workers. The process goes on until unemployment is completely absorbed.

In theory, unemployment disappears for two reasons: a reduction of wages reduces firms' production costs and therefore induces them to expand production. To do this they need to employ other workers. Furthermore, if a commodity can be produced with different techniques, when salaries are reduced, firms are driven to adopt techniques that use more labour and less capital. Thus there is always an *equilibrium wage*, that makes labour demand and supply equal. No involuntary unemployment may exist, because whoever wants to work may always do so, provided he is not asking for a wage higher than the equilibrium one. Consequently, underemployment equilibria cannot exist. Rather, there are automatic forces within the economy that ensure full employment. As we have seen, these forces are represented by the variations of the prices of goods and the variations of wages.

2.3 THE INCOME MULTIPLIER AND THE KEYNESIAN THEORY OF EMPLOYMENT

The pre-Keynesian theory of employment remained within the neoclassical school: economists, whether reasoning in microeconomic or macroeconomic terms, maintained that price and wage flexibility would always automatically lead the economy to full employment. This argument, still dominant in the Thirties was, however, unable to explain the Great Depression that occurred in those years and was particularly destructive. In the early Thirties investments and production in the main industrial economies, i.e. in Britain and the United States, had a slump, while unemployment soared even though prices were falling. The slump, in varying degrees of intensity, spread rapidly throughout all European countries. The most striking phenomenon was that mass unemployment did not occur in underdeveloped countries such as India but, rather, it was particularly high in the most advanced countries and in industry, where firms could not manage to sell the goods they produced and therefore contracted their production and investment, went bankrupt and laid off workers.

From the observation of this fact, Keynes criticised the traditional approach. He maintained that wages are not flexible downwards because trade unions do not let them fall below a given level, which they believe represents the minimum acceptable level. Therefore, when there are unemployed workers in an economy, if wages cannot fall, it is possible to have an underemployment equilibrium, namely a level of production and effective income lower than the potential one.

Keynes went beyond this, maintaining that, even if wages are able to fall freely, full employment will not be reached. In fact, he thought that a reduction of wages would cause workers' demand for consumer goods to fall. Firms, experiencing a decrease in demand, would curtail the production of goods and services and thus lay off workers. In this way there would be a fall in both income (i.e. production) and employment. The reduction of wages, far from representing a remedy for unemployment, would cause it to increase.

Keynes made a further comment: in a situation where unemployed workers and idle plant are present, as in the Thirties, the behaviour of firms needs to be carefully analysed. How does a firm behave when the demand for its goods is greater than the quantity it offers (i.e. it supplies)? If there are unemployed workers and idle machinery in the economy the firm does not raise the price of the commodity (as neoclassical economists maintained), but expands production to satisfy the greater demand. Only if the economy is in full employment then the firm cannot expand production, i.e. supply, and raises prices.

At the macroeconomic level this means that, when the system is in a situation of underemployment, an excess of total demand over total supply causes an increase in production, i.e. in national income. Only when the system is in full employment, an excess in total demand over total supply determines an increase in prices. Similarly, if total supply exceeds total demand in underemployment, that is, if firms cannot sell part of their production, they curtail production rather than prices. When total supply exceeds total demand, there is said to be a scarcity of the latter.

Consequently, in underemployment the level of total supply (i.e. of production, or of actual national income) is determined by the level of total demand. It is therefore necessary to examine what determines the level of total demand: it certainly cannot be prices because, as we have seen, in underemployment prices do not vary.

The answer to this question is given by the theory of the *income multiplier*, which was first formulated by the British economist Kahn and then taken up by Keynes.

Let us assume a situation where there is idle machinery and unemployed workers and suppose the state or a private firm makes an investment: for example, it constructs a road or a building.

To do this, the state or the firm employs workers who were previously unemployed, paying them a certain wage. Suppose the state or the firm employs ten workers and gives each of them two thousand pounds per year, thus creating an income of twenty thousand pounds. If previously the ten workers received no unemployment benefit, national income rises by twenty thousand pounds.

The workers who receive this income spend part of it (namely, they use it to buy consumer goods) and save part of it. Suppose they spend half of it (equal to ten thousand pounds) and save the other half and that they use the first ten thousand pounds to buy bread, meat and clothes. The demand for these goods therefore rises.

The firms producing bread, meat and clothes raise supply to meet the higher demand and, to do so, they hire unemployed workers and start using the machines that were previously idle. Since there is underemployment, firms respond to the increase in demand by expanding production and not by raising prices. In our example the firms that produce bread, meat and clothes collect ten thousand pounds from higher sales and distribute this sum as income to the agents taking part in production. With that sum they pay the wages of the newly employed workers, the interest to those from whom they have received loans, etc. and they keep the rest, namely profit.

Consequently, the part of the higher income that is spent in the first phase (ten thousand pounds) becomes the income of the agents that take part in production in the second phase. Thus the income generated in this process is no longer twenty thousand pounds, but rather 20,000 + 10,000 = 30,000. Up to this point national income has therefore risen by thirty thousand pounds.

The process goes on. Those who received ten thousand pounds as an income spend part of it on consumer goods and save part of it. Again, let us assume that half the income, i.e. five thousand pounds, will be spent to buy goods. Thus five thousand pounds become a revenue for other firms that, to keep up with the rise of the demand for goods, expand production, hiring more unemployed people. The five thousand pounds thus become an income for workers and other economic agents (people receiving interest, dividends, etc.) who receive this sum from firms.

From the beginning of the process the income generated is equal to £20,000 + 10,000 + 5,000 = £35,000. The process goes on. A simple mathematical formula indicates how much income is generated from an initial investment. Here suffice it to say that, through the multiplier process described, an initial investment produces an increase of income and employment that is much greater than the initial investment itself.

From our example it appears clear that, if in the first phase workers save all the income they are given (this is obviously unrealistic), no multiplier effect takes place. If, instead, the income distributed to workers and to the other economic agents in all the phases is always spent completely, the multiplier process, namely the creation of new income and of new employment, continues indefinitely[3] and stops only when the economy reaches full employment (both for plant and people). At that point, even if the demand for goods increases, firms are unable to expand production further, so that the process of creating new income comes to an end.

It is obvious that the income and the employment generated by the multiplier process is greater, the greater the amount of income spent on consumer goods by the agents receiving new income. In the example we have seen that the subjects who receive income spend part and save part of it. The part (fraction, percentage) of newly created income that is spent on consumption goods is called *marginal propensity to consume*. In our example it is equal to fifty per cent. For the economy as a whole the marginal propensity to consume is given by the ratio between the increase of consumption (of the whole country) and the increase of national income. If, for instance, total consumption increases by eighty million pounds when national income increases by 100 million, the marginal propensity to consume is equal to:

$$80,000,000/100,000,000 = 0.80 = 80\%.[4]$$

The higher the initial investment and the marginal propensity to consume, the more income (demand for goods) and thus production and employment is created. Consequently two factors determine the level of a country's actual national income (i.e. of income actually produced): the volume of investment and the value of the marginal propensity to consume of the public as a whole. The actual national income thus determined is also called equilibrium national income because it makes total demand equal to total supply.

The problem then arises as to whether the volume of investment and the value of the marginal propensity to consume are in general high enough to ensure a level of national income equal to the potential one, a level, in other words, that guarantees full employment of the resources.

Keynes maintains that actual income is usually lower than potential income. In fact, the volume of investments depends on two factors: firms' expectations with regard to market demand and profits, and the interest rate.

If firms expect demand for the goods they produce to grow, ensuring high profits, they invest. But, according to Keynes, for various reasons forecasts are often pessimistic and firms consequently make few investments.

On the other hand, the interest rate represents the cost of credit, namely the sum a firm has to pay a bank in order to obtain a loan for financing investments. The lower the interest rate, the higher the volume of investment, all other circumstances being equal. Yet in many cases the interest rate may not be low enough to generate a level of investments which in turn, through the multiplier, leads to a volume of national income that ensures full employment.

Furthermore, countries with a high level of average income (Keynes had in mind the United Kingdom and the United States), have marginal propensities to consume which are fairly low. This means that when individuals who already have a high income get a rise of income, they save a large part of it rather than consuming it.

An inadequate volume of investment coupled with a low marginal propensity to consume generates a volume of national income which is below that of potential one. For Keynes, therefore, industrial countries, where individuals have a high level of income, tend to have unemployment, stagnating in an underemployment equilibrium. Contrary to what neoclassical economists thought, for Keynes there are no forces endogenous to the economy that tend automatically to achieve full employment, given that in modern industrial economies neither prices nor wages are flexible downwards. Furthermore, even if wages were flexible, Keynes argued that a fall of wages, far from representing a remedy for unemployment, would worsen it.

2.4 KEYNESIAN ECONOMIC POLICY

For Keynes, the mechanism outlined above explained the high and persistent unemployment of industrial economies in the Thirties. We will see later that Keynes' analysis becomes more far-reaching when monetary factors are introduced. However, it is possible to trace precise economic policy patterns even from this analysis alone.

Given that there is no automatic mechanism ensuring full employment, state intervention is necessary to raise the volume of investment and the marginal propensity to consume in order to guarantee a job for everyone. An increase in investment and the marginal propensity to consume, through the multiplier, raises both national income and employment.

The marginal propensity to consume can be raised in different ways: for instance, by lowering taxes on consumer goods, by reducing the cost of hire-purchase for these goods, and, finally, by redistributing income from the rich to the poor, i.e. imposing a progressive taxation that affects the former more than the latter. When the poor receive an increase in income, they spend a large fraction of it on consumer goods, while the rich already have a high level of consumption so that when they receive an increase in income, they spend only a small part of it on consumption. In other words, the marginal propensity to consume is much higher for the poor than the rich, thus a redistribution of income from the latter to the former increases the marginal propensity to consume of the community as a whole.

However, Keynes maintains that redistributive measures of this kind are met by strong political and social resistance. A similar resistance occurs for programmes that expand public consumption extensively, such as expenditure on education, health, etc., given that programmes of this type require heavy increases in taxation.[5]

Given the difficulties of raising the marginal propensity to consume, Keynes advocates the necessity of taking measures to increase investment. In the first place, it is necessary to stimulate private investment by improving entrepreneurs' expectations. One way of doing this is to raise public orders to private firms. For example, if the state or local authorities purchase trains, buses, etc. from private companies, these have a higher demand for their goods, and therefore raise investment. Another way of stimulating firms' investments is to reduce the cost of credit or taxes for firms.

These measures however may still prove to be inadequate. Even a strong reduction in firms' costs may not induce them to invest if expectations remain extremely pessimistic. In this case the state must invest directly in public works: for example, by constructing roads, railways, houses, etc. For Keynes, the fundamental way to reach full employment is to implement public investment.

NOTES

1. In the United Kingdom the state represents the consolidated activities of the public sector as a whole. Therefore, it includes the central government and local authorities. In order to have a more complete idea of the public sector's activities, public corporations and corporate bodies also need to be considered, including subsidiaries that are both owned and controlled by the government on a basis that is intended as permanent.
2. For example, if the Treasury buys a computer,in national accounts this is classified as a public investment, while if the same computer is bought by a private enterprise it is classified as a private investment.
3. In such an instance in our example income generated would be 40,000.000 + 40,000.000 + 40,000.000 + ... That is, in each phase a volume of income is created that is equal to the amount created in the previous one. Instead, if not all the income is spent, the volume of income created in each phase becomes gradually smaller.
4. Note that the *marginal propensity to consume* usually has a different value from the *average propensity to consume*, since the latter is given by the ratio between total consumption and national income. For example, in 1990 the national income of a country is 100 million pounds and total consumption 90 million;

the following year (1991) national income increases by one million pounds, reaching 101 million, while total consumption increases by 0.8 million, thus reaching 90.8 million. In this case the average propensity to consume in 1990 is:

$$90,000,000/100,000,000 = 0.9 = 90\%$$

and in 1991:

$$90,800,000/101,000,000 = 0.899 = 89.9\%.$$

The marginal propensity to consume (between the two years) is

$$\frac{90,800,000}{101,000,000} - \frac{90,000,000}{100,000,000} = \frac{800,000}{1,000,000} = 0.8 = 80\% \ .$$

The marginal propensity to consume is a ratio between increments, and can therefore only be calculated if data relative to two consecutive years are available.

5. Many of these arguments, which were formulated in the Thirties, have lost relevance, given the changes in people's mentality and in the power relations among different social groups in industrial countries.

3 The debate on the role of money: the theory of the demand for money

3.1 THE QUANTITY THEORY OF MONEY

Keynes' contribution is also very important in the field of monetary analysis. However, to grasp it completely, it is necessary to go back to the theory dominant in the Thirties. This was the so called *quantity theory of money*, already anticipated in the Sixteenth century by various scholars, including the French economist Bodin, but formulated rigorously only at the end of the last century by the American economist Irving Fisher.

According to this theory, a rise in the quantity of money in circulation leads to a rise in the general price level and thus reduces the value of money, namely its purchasing power.

In several instances in the past a big expansion of the quantity of money caused a notable rise in the general price level. The examples most frequently quoted are the events following the discovery of America and the situation of Germany just after the end of the First World War.

Immediately after the discovery of America large quantities of precious metals (gold and silver) were imported into Europe. Since gold and silver coins were then in circulation and the right to coin was in force, allowing any individual to take gold to the mint and exchange it for coins, the importation of large quantities of precious metals caused a great expansion of the money in circulation. A similar phenomenon occurred in Germany at the end of the First World War, when the central German bank printed paper money to finance war expenditures and thus raised the money in circulation enormously.

The main idea of the quantity theory of money in its various formulations is that the money introduced into the economy ends up in the hands of individuals (consumers or firms) who spend it to purchase goods. Consequently, a rise in the quantity of money gives rise to an expansion of the demand for goods (consumer goods from consumers and investment goods, plant and machinery from firms). If the economy is in full employment such that production, i.e. the supply of goods, cannot be expanded, the increase in demand induces firms to raise their prices. If, on the other hand, there are unemployed workers and idle machinery, the increase in demand induces firms to expand production.

Suppose for instance that the government increases the salaries of civil servants and, to do this, it prints new money. The latter, when given to economic agents, is spent on consumer goods. The result, as we have seen, is either a rise in the price of these goods or an expansion of production.

3.2 THE KEYNESIAN THEORY OF THE DEMAND FOR MONEY

Although the previous result may seem at first sight obvious and indisputable, things may actually be different. Individuals receiving money (in the example above, civil servants), may not spend it, but hoard it or deposit it in a bank. In this case, the rise in the quantity of money would not cause an increase in demand and would thus have no effect on prices or on the level of production. It is true that, if individuals deposit the money at a bank, banks have more money and could therefore grant more loans to firms, possibly at a lower cost (i.e. a lower interest rate). Given that if many individuals wish to deposit money at banks, these may reduce the interest rate on deposits and consequently that on loans to firms. This, in turn, could induce firms to raise investment. The demand for investment goods of some firms would thus increase and this, as we have seen in the previous chapter, would generate an increase of income and production through the multiplier. However, the latter would not be a direct effect of the rise of the quantity of money on global demand but rather an indirect effect, as it takes place only through the banking system and the variation of the interest rate.

It follows that, according to Keynes, a rise in the quantity of money does not necessarily or automatically cause an increase in total demand (for goods and services), as maintained by the quantity theory of money. The level of expenditure (namely total demand) depends in practice on the propensity of different subjects to spend: on consumers' propensity to consume and on firms' propensity to invest. While for the quantity theory of money there is a fixed ratio between the quantity of money in the economy and individuals' expenditure and thus between the quantity of money and the total demand for goods and services, for Keynes there is no fixed ratio.

Keynes' analysis, however, goes beyond these considerations. As we have argued, when individuals receive money, they can either spend it or hold it (at home or putting it in a bank). Let us consider an individual with a monthly income of £800 and suppose that £600 is spent on consumer goods. What happens to the £200 that are saved? They may be kept liquid (at home or in a bank) or they may be used (in part or entirely) to purchase bonds, shares, an apartment, etc. Money, therefore, is not only a means of exchange to purchase goods as the quantity theory of money implicitly maintains, but it is also one of the many ways in which income (or wealth or savings) may be held.

An analysis of the effects of a rise in the quantity of money on total demand and consequently on production and prices therefore requires an examination of the motives that drive individuals to keep larger or smaller parts of their income in the form of money (namely, in cash or in the form of bank deposits) rather than in other forms (bonds, shares, etc.). This is the problem of the demand for money.

Keynes examined the motives that induce individuals to hold a part of their income in the form of money (or, in technical terms, to demand money) and considered three different purposes: the transactions motive, the precautionary motive and the speculative motive.

Every time an individual buys goods or services, he has to pay for them and therefore he must have a certain amount of money: this is the transactions motive. Moreover, during a lifetime an individual may be obliged to face unexpected expenses, due to illness, injuries, etc. Individuals, therefore, keep money for a precautionary motive.

According to Keynes the demand for money (that is, the quantity of money desired) for these two motives depends on the agent's level of income. In general, the higher a person's income, the more expensive the goods and services he purchases and thus the larger the quantity of money held to pay for them and to face unexpected payments. On the other hand, the speculative demand for money depends on the interest rate. To avoid any confusion, it is best to specify at once what rate is intended here. In the world that Keynes considered, that is Britain and the United States in the Thirties, the most important interest rate was that paid on bonds (especially government stocks such as Treasury bills, gilt-edged and national savings), while banks paid no interest on current account deposits.

In an industrial economy, where financial institutions are specialised, individuals can hold the income that they do not consume (namely, that they save) in different forms (money, shares, bonds, real estate, etc.). For simplicity, however, Keynes only considered two options for keeping money: it could be either kept liquid or used to buy bonds.

An individual keeping his income liquid (either cash or deposited in a current account) has no return on it but has the advantage of being able to spend it immediately. On the other hand, a subject that invests his income in bonds earns a profit equal to the yield (that is, the interest rate) produced by the bond, but loses the advantage of having a liquid sum at his disposal. In fact, an individual having to make a payment must first sell his bonds to get cash. Since the price of bonds fluctuates according to demand and supply just like the price of goods, he may be forced to sell his bonds at a price lower than that he paid for them, suffering losses that are called 'capital losses'. The fact that a risk of incurring in capital losses occurs makes bonds and any other form of holding income (shares, property, etc.) different from money. The fact that money is liquid (i.e. immediately spendable) means that it is free from risk.[1]

The higher the interest rate, the stronger the incentive for individuals to invest their income in bonds rather than keeping it in the form of money, and thus the smaller the demand for money.

To understand this point one must consider the relation between the interest rate and the price of a bond.

A bond has a nominal value that is written on it: let us assume that it is of one pound. The price at which the bond is sold when it is issued is often lower than the nominal value, but for simplicity let us assume that the nominal value and the issue price are the same. Bonds give a fixed interest rate while shares produce variable returns acccording to the dividend that the issuing society distributes.[2]

Suppose, therefore, that a bond with a nominal value (and issue price) of one pound gives an annual interest of ten pence. This income remains identical throughout the life of the bond, while the price (or the quotation) at which it can be bought or sold varies according to the demand and supply of bonds.

Suppose that the demand for bonds from the public increases. This causes an increase in the price of our bond, which for instance passes from £1.00 to £1.25. The bond still yields 10 pence a year, but 10 pence is 10 per cent of £1.00, while it is only 8 per cent of £1.25.[3]

Thus, since a bond gives a fixed income, an increase in its price causes a fall in its yield rate, i.e. of its interest rate. On the other hand, a fall in a bond's price (due to a decrease of demand for bonds) causes an increase in its interest rate.

If the price of bonds is high (greater than what economic agents believe to be the normal price) and thus the interest rate is low, individuals sell their bonds at once and delay purchases until prices have gone down. In this situation, therefore, economic agents hold large quantities of cash to purchase bonds in the future at more favourable rates. If vice versa the price of bonds is low (below the normal price) and thus the interest rate is high, individuals purchase securities at once and postpone selling the bonds they possess until prices become higher. In this situation individuals hold little cash and large amounts of securities.

In conclusion, holding (namely, demanding for) money for speculative purposes depends on the interest rate. When the latter rises, speculative demand for money falls; when the interest rate decreases, the demand for money for speculative purposes increases.

Furthermore, for Keynes the interest rate never falls below a given value, around two per cent. When the interest rate reaches this value, the price of bonds is so high (with respect to its normal price) that individuals assume that it must necessarily fall soon. Consequently they do not buy bonds, but they wait for their price to fall, and hold all the income they do not consume in the form of money. The yield of bonds is considered by Keynes to be like a premium for giving up liquidity; when it is too low, individuals do not forgo the advantages of keeping their incomes liquid. Keynes calls the minimum value of the interest rate the *liquidity trap*.

In conclusion, for Keynes, the demand for money is given by the sum of the demand for money for transactions, for precautionary motives and for speculative motives. While the first two rise as income rises, the second increases when the interest rate goes down.

Keynes' fundamental contribution to the theory of the demand for money is in having brought attention to the fact that money does not only serve as a *medium of exchange* but also as a *store of value* and a *reserve of liquidity*. This idea was new in the Anglo-Saxon world, while on the continent it had already been considered some decades before Keynes by Walras and by other economists.

According to the quantity theory, money is only a medium of exchange. In modern societies, where the expansion of trade is so vast, a single instrument for making payments is necessary and this is money. Individuals therefore wish to hold a part of their income in the form of money only for transactions. Since people are paid monthly but purchase goods – and thus make payments – every day, it is necessary for them to hold money. If the motive for holding money is a lack of synchronisation, i.e. a time lag between receipts and payments, and if the lag remains constant over time (because firms' habits concerning the time of payment of salaries and wages do not change, nor do the habits of individuals concerning the time of purchases), it can be assumed that the money desired by individuals is a constant fraction of their income and thus that there is a constant ratio between the quantity of money and expenditure (that is, total demand or income).

Keynes called attention to the fact that money is also a means for storing value. Individuals can hold the income they save (i.e. they do not consume) in different forms (shares, bonds, real estate, etc.) and one of these is money. Furthermore, money has a characteristic that none of the other forms of holding income have: liquidity. Individuals can transform other assets (shares, bonds, real estate) that they own into money by selling them but, at the moment of selling them, they face the risk of losses.

Money, unlike other assets, yields no interest but is liquid. Keynes made a gross oversimplification by considering only two forms in which income can be held: money and bonds. This consideration, however, is enough to reject the hypothesis that individuals immediately spend the money they receive purchasing goods. In fact, whether money is spent or not depends also on individuals' expectations on interest rate trends, namely on the price of bonds. The latter changes according to individuals' demand and supply of bonds, which, in turn, depend on their (pessimistic or optimistic) expectations, which are generally unpredictable. Consequently, the conclusions of the quantity theory whereby any sum of money given to individuals is immediately transformed into an increase in demand for goods are to be rejected.

Keynes, moreover, considered the experience of the Great Depression, when money was not spent. To understand the reason for this phenomenon it should be remembered that the crisis of the Thirties was characterised by the prevalence of pessimistic expectations on behalf of entrepreneurs concerning the demand for the goods they produced. Firms therefore reduced investment and laid off workers, causing unemployment to rise. The demand for consumer goods fell even more, since many workers were deprived of their income. Production and employment fell further: the drop in total demand pushed the economy towards a recession. Firms tried to improve the situation by reducing prices, thus hoping to expand sales. They could do this because they could curtail workers' wages, given that the latter accepted lower earnings, for fear of losing their jobs (the power of the trade unions was very weak in those years). Thus a situation was created where investment, total demand, production and employment fell, as well as wages and prices. This contrasts with the experience of the Seventies, when unemployment and inflation (in the form of increasing wages and prices) coexisted in most industrial economies (this is the case of stagflation, which will be discussed in chapter six).

In the Thirties, when prices were stable or even falling, individuals did not fear a loss in the purchasing power of money and so they held a large portion of their incomes in the form of money. This also happened because the interest rate (on bonds) was very low, near the value of the liquidity trap, and thus the price of securities was very high, and individuals did not buy bonds. On the other hand, firms did not invest, i.e. they did not purchase raw materials to be transformed into finished products, nor did they buy new plant and machinery, because the expectations on demand were pessimistic: firms felt that they would not be able to sell all their products.

It is obvious that in such a situation, if the state had created money to finance the payment of unemployment benefits, this would probably have caused a rise in the demand for goods by the unemployed and a consequent expansion of production by firms. The authorities, however, were unwilling to pursue an outright policy of income redistribution to the benefit of the poor. Instead they created money by purchasing securities from private individuals (the so called *open market operations*). Private savers sold their securities to the monetary authorities, given that the latter were prepared to purchase them at a high price. However, once they received money in exchange, they deposited it at a bank: that is, they held their savings in the form of money rather than in the form of bonds. It results clearly that an increase in the quantity of money produced in this way did not cause an increase in the demand for consumer goods. Nor could the larger bank deposits and the consequent reduction of interest rates on deposits and on loans (of banks to firms) lead firms to expand production and investments, given their pessimistic expectations on future sales. Consequently, the therapy suggested by Keynes against the crisis consisted, as we have seen, in a state intervention to raise public investment and to stimulate private investment (thus absorbing unemployment and giving an income to the unemployed, who would spend it on consumer goods, stimulating in this way the expansion of production) and to increase families' propensity to consume.

3.3 SOME DEVELOPMENTS IN THE THEORY OF THE DEMAND FOR MONEY: FRIEDMAN'S ANALYSIS AND THE PORTFOLIO APPROACH

The Keynesian theory of the demand for money was influenced by the context in which Keynes wrote, namely the situation of the Thirties, which was characterised by a fall in investment, in total demand, in production and in employment, but also by the stability or even the fall in the prices of goods. A few years later, with the outbreak of the Second World War (1939-1945), the economic situation of the main industrial countries changed radically. The war made it necessary to produce large quantities of war material and other goods, so that state expenditure for these purposes brought total demand to the level of full employment income. The pressure of demand over total supply in the presence of full employment resulted in an increase in the prices of goods, i.e. in inflation, given that production could not increase further. In inflation individuals, seeing that money loses its purchasing power, try to get rid of it by buying goods. They therefore buy buildings, gold, stocks of consumer goods; firms immediately buy raw materials and production equipment, expecting prices to go up. Consequently, both individuals and firms hold little money.

Economists therefore began to ask themselves whether Keynesian theory was not limited to a particular situation and they began to reconsider the theory of the demand for money.

Milton Friedman, an American economist of the Chicago, or 'monetarist', school, undertook many empirical studies to verify whether in practice there is or not a stable relation between the quantity of money and individuals' expenditure (namely income or total demand for goods and services).

Friedman's studies, relating both to the United States and to other countries in different periods of time, show that the relationship between the quantity of money and expenditure is variable in the short term, while it is fairly stable in the long run. In the short term, however, Friedman maintains that the relationship does not vary in an unpredictable way, as Keynes stated, but according to a stable rule.

In recession, for the reasons we have seen, if prices are stable or decreasing, individuals hold a large part of their income in the form of money.

During an expansion, investment, production and employment increase. If unemployed resources are present in the economy, the prices of goods remain stable. Firms, which have optimistic expectations, need money to invest (that is, to purchase raw materials, plant and machinery). They get money also by issuing shares and bonds and by getting individuals to buy them through the distribution of high dividends and granting a high interest rate on bonds. In this situation individuals purchase both securities and goods, and hold only a small part of their income in the form of money.

The reason pushing people to hold little money in inflationary periods has already been analysed. For the same reasons, individuals also get rid of money in periods in which an increase in prices coexists with unemployment, a phenomenon known as 'stagflation'. This occurred in recent years in industrial countries and will be dealt with later.

In the long term, on the other hand, for Friedman the relationship between the quantity of money and expenditure is fairly stable, so that, as we shall see, increases in the quantity of money in circulation can lead to increases in the price level (if the economy is in full employment and therefore production cannot be expanded) or to increases in production (if there are unemployed resources in the economy).

Friedman was not entirely satisfied with these investigations, so he and other economists (including, among the others, Tobin from the United States and Allais from France) further examined the laws which explain the behaviour of the demand for money. They began by considering Keynes' basic point, that money is one of the forms in which people may hold their incomes. Furthermore, they did not limit their analysis to individuals' income but extended it to their wealth. The latter can be held in various forms: money, bonds, shares, land, buildings, etc. Individuals distribute their wealth among these different forms of investment according to the yield that each gives and the risks of losses that are incurred in investing in each of them. They distribute wealth so as to maximise the flow of returns they get from these investments. Tobin termed the problem as the determination of the individual's 'optimal portfolio decisions'.[4] Thus the demand for money of an individual depends upon his wealth, his preferences for the various forms of investment and the yield of each of these.

Given the difficulty of measuring wealth statistically, Friedman uses income as a proxy for it. However he considers income not over a single year, but rather permanent income, that is a person's average income calculated over a period of several years, an income to be considered as normal for a fairly long period of time.

Friedman also insists upon the fact that individuals value the quantity of money they wish to hold (namely, the demand for money) not in nominal but in real terms, that is, in terms of the actual purchasing power of money. Thus, if prices of goods go up, the demand for money from individuals will also increase, given that a larger quantity of money is needed to buy the same amount of goods.

Friedman and his supporters undertook numerous empirical investigations from which, in their view, it results that there is a relation that remains stable over time between the demand for money and the factors influencing it (mentioned above). Nevertheless, since these statistical results do not have an univocal interpretation, this conclusion cannot be said to be unequivocally proven.

NOTES

1. This is true as Keynes considers a situation in which the prices of goods are stable (there is no inflation), so money does not lose its purchasing power over time.
2. In periods of inflation, when prices of goods go up, companies and the state issue indexed bonds, which are bonds with a variable yield, linked to the rate of inflation. This will be discussed in chapter six. The Keynesian analysis we are dealing with is based on the hypothesis that the prices of goods are stable (in other words, there is no inflation): this, moreover, was the situation in the Thirties, when there were only fixed yield bonds.
3. In fact, $10:125 = 0.08 = 8/100 = 8\%$.
4. Tobin only considers financial assets: shares, bonds and other forms of securities.

4 The role and the effects of monetary policy

4.1 THE CHANNELS THROUGH WHICH MONEY IS INTRODUCED INTO THE ECONOMY

One of the themes that is subject to most discussion in current economic theory concerns the effect of variations in the quantity of money in circulation, that is the effect of monetary policy,on investment, national income and prices. In order to examine these problems in detail, we need to make some considerations about the channels through which money is created, i.e. how it is introduced into the economy.

Until now we have considered the reasons which lead an agent to hold part of his income in the form of money (demand for money); now we need to explore how the money supply is determined, or how money is created.

In most countries there is a central bank or monetary agency (for example, the Bank of England) which prints notes and introduces them into the economy.

In the past the central bank owned some gold reserves; moreover, notes were convertible into gold on the basis of the parity decided by the bank itself. The Bank of England, for instance, assessed that one pound was equivalent to two ounces of gold and anyone presenting a pound note to the Bank of England received in return that specified amount of gold and vice versa. In such a system the central bank issued notes only when it had sufficient reserves of gold to convert them (upon request). Thus, the quantity of paper money in circulation was proportional to the gold reserves held by the central bank.

Today, however, this system has in practice disappeared, as notes are no longer convertible into gold. Monetary authorities decide the quantity of money to be supplied according to their economic policy goals. When prices increase (inflation) they reduce money creation, while during a crisis (low investment, low aggregate demand, etc.) the authorities expand the quantity of money thereby hoping to stimulate both investment and national income. Money created by the central bank is introduced into the economy through four channels: central bank-Treasury relations, central bank-banking system relations, open market operations, the balance of payments.

When the state spends more than its revenue (taxation and other revenue), the Treasury may finance the deficit (the difference between expenditure and revenue) by means of money collected by issuing Treasury securities. When such bonds are purchased by the private sector (families or firms), there is no increase of money in circulation, but merely a transfer from these agents to the Treasury. Conversely, if the private sector is reluctant to purchase such bonds, the Treasury asks the central bank to buy them. In this manner the latter lends to the former money which was not previously in circulation, hence the quantity of money in the economy increases. The central bank can also lend money to the Treasury through another channel, given by the fact that in almost every country the Treasury enjoys at least one current account with the central bank on which it can issue cheques (generally within certain limits), thereby creating money. Rather than being a current account, this is a line of credit of the central bank in favour of the Treasury, through which new money is created.

The second channel of money creation is found in the relations between the central bank and commercial banks. Such relations consist of several operations among which the major ones are advances and rediscount. The former are the loans made by the central bank to commercial banks (which, in their turn, lend money to firms). For these loans commercial banks pay the central bank an interest rate which is fixed by the central bank and is called the *interest rate on advances*. It is through these loans that the central bank introduces new money into the economy.

37

Another operation that takes place between the central bank and commercial banks is the rediscount of exchange bills. Assume that an individual has a bill that is due to mature after two months. He has a credit against someone, but it is collectable only after two months. He can take such a bill to a bank, which gives him a sum of money equivalent to that promised in the bill, less a percentage as interest payment for the bank itself.[1] This operation is called discount and the rate charged for this operation is the *discount rate*. Through this operation the commercial banks own bills which may, in turn, be discounted by the central bank. This is the same operation, but when it is made between a commercial bank and the central bank it is called rediscount and the rate applied is called the *rediscount rate* or *intervention rate*. Rediscount operations create money since they envisage the central bank giving commercial banks new money in exchange for bills.

The third channel of money creation is *open market operations*, which consist in the sale or purchase of securities by the central bank. When the bank buys bills from the private sector it gives money in exchange, thus introducing new money into the system.

The fourth channel is the *balance of payments*. For example, an Englishman who exports commodities is paid in dollars. He may wish to sell dollars to the Exchange Equalization Account (through which the Bank of England enters transactions with the foreign exchange market) and receive pounds in exchange. Through these means new money is introduced into the economy. Conversely, the same mechanism leads imports to cause money destruction. A surplus of the balance of payments determines money creation; conversely, a deficit destroys money.[2]

4.2 THE DEPOSIT MULTIPLIER AND THE MONETARY BASE

As we have seen, the central bank creates money through four channels. Commercial banks cannot create money, but can multiply it. The point will be illustrated by means of a simple example.

By law, in many countries every bank has to deposit in the central bank a percentage of its deposits, called *compulsory reserve ratio*. Let us suppose that it amounts to twenty per cent and let us consider an individual depositing 100 pounds in a bank.

The bank deposits twenty pounds in the central bank and grants a loan of eighty pounds to an entreprise or to some other agent. Those receiving the eighty pounds loan are not likely to keep it, but rather they deposit it in the same or in another bank, also because they make their payments through cheques. However, after circulating among individuals, the eighty pounds return, at least in part, to the banking system. For the sake of simplicity, let us assume that all the eighty pounds return to the banks. Again, the latter deposit twenty per cent of eighty pounds in the central bank and lend the remaining part (eighty per cent of eighty pounds = sixty four pounds). Let us assume that these sixty four pounds return again to the banking system and that the process goes on.

From the initial deposit of 100 pounds several successive deposits are generated. The global amount of deposits turns out to be:

$$100 + 80 + 64 + ...$$

The final amount of deposits generated from a given initial deposit obviously depends upon the value of the compulsory reserve ratio. If it were equal to 100 per cent, banks could not multiply deposits. If, instead, it were zero percent, banks' capacity of multiplying the initial deposit would be unlimited. In general, the higher the compulsory reserve ratio the lower the amount of deposits generated from a given initial deposit.

Until now we have assumed that the compulsory ratio is constituted by cash only. However, in most countries banks are allowed to deposit at the central bank not only cash but also state securities or other types of securities. Following the previous example, let us assume that a bank has received a 100 pounds deposit from a customer and deposits twenty as its compulsory reserve in the central bank. The central bank then decides that this reserve can be paid, other than through cash, through Treasury securities. Since the latter yields an interest rate higher than that one the central bank pays to commercial banks on the sums deposited as compulsory reserves, the bank finds it convenient to buy Treasury securities and to deposit them as a reserve instead of cash.

If the quantity of outstanding Treasury securities has a total value given by the issuing price of a security multiplied by the number of securities of ten pounds, the bank withdraws ten pounds from its reserves, purchases Treasury securities for that amount and deposits them as a reserve. In this way, the amount of ten pounds which was frozen in the compulsory reserve is given to the Treasury, which spends it for its payments, and hence it enters again in circulation. Individuals receiving it may deposit it in a bank and, then, it is subject again to the multiplicative process described earlier.

Hence, the sum of money subject to multiplication is not formed only by the economy's cash (100 pounds), but by cash plus a value equivalent to the quantity of outstanding securities which can be deposited as reserves (100 + 10).

Cash and all the securities depositable as compulsory reserves constitute the *monetary base*, which is subject to multiplication.

4.3 MONETARY POLICY INSTRUMENTS

The concept of monetary base was introduced into economic analysis after the Second World War and it represents a refinement of the money supply theory. Empirical evidence shows that a change in the monetary base affects investment, national income and prices. The most recent analyses have led to further refinements of the concept of monetary base. In the following discussion we shall use the terms 'monetary base' and 'quantity (or supply) of money' indifferently.

The quantity of money in circulation may be reduced or augmented by different ways related to the channels through which it is introduced into the economy.

To reduce the monetary base created by the relationship between the central bank and the Treasury it is necessary to persuade the private sector to purchase a larger quantity of Treasury bonds (for example, by increasing their yield). Alternatively the public deficit is reduced by either decreasing public expenditure or by increasing revenues (both tax and other revenues).

As far as the second channel is concerned, an increase of the intervention rate reduces the creation of monetary base. In practice, such an increase makes the banks raise the discount rate: for, if they did not do so, they would have to bear a loss. The number of bills which customers discount with banks would accordingly be reduced and the banks, in turn, would rediscount a smaller number of bills with the central bank. Hence, the quantity of money created would be reduced. Similar effects would be produced by an increase in the interest rate which banks pay to the central bank on the advances the latter grants them. Such an increase leads banks to curtail their use of advances and through this way money creation is reduced. All these policies imply a higher cost of both rediscount and advance. The central bank, however, may produce the same effect by directly reducing the amount of bills rediscounted or the amount of money advanced (that is, lent) directly to commercial banks.

As we have already seen, open market operations either create or destroy money, depending on whether the central bank purchases or sells bonds to the private sector.

Finally, the policies which cause an increase of exports of commodities and services or an inflow of foreign capitals create money, while those which cause an increase of imports or an outflow of capitals destroy money.

The instruments analysed until now affect the creation of the monetary base on behalf of the central bank. The latter may change banks' reserve ratio: such a policy does not affect the creation of the monetary base, but rather the capacity of the banking system to multiply it. An increase of the ratio, as we have already seen, reduces this capacity, while a reduction of the ratio increases it.

Rather than changing the reserve ratio, monetary authorities can change its composition, allowing banks to satisfy the requirement partly through public securities rather than through cash. The fact that more bonds are allowed to be deposited as a reserve produces an expansion of the monetary base with effects which are similar to an increase in the quantity of money.

Finally, authorities may implement administrative policies inducing banks to expand loans to firms operating in some sector rather than in another; similarly, banks may discriminate according to the firms' size in order, for instance, to favour the small ones. Such measures, representing a selective credit policy, do not affect the entire money supply but rather its redistribution among firms and sectors in the economy. Empirical evidence, however, shows that the effects of such policies are quite small.

4.4 A COMPARISON BETWEEN THE QUANTITY THEORY OF MONEY AND THE KEYNESIAN MULTIPLIER

Before analysing the effects of a change in the quantity of money on investments, national income, etc., some additional consideration is needed. National income and its components (consumption, investment, exports) are called *real magnitudes* since they are quantities of commodities and services. Although they are expressed in monetary terms (for example, in 1989 national income in Britain amounted to 508,859 million pounds), money is just a *means of measurement* of these magnitudes. Actually, as heterogenous goods cannot be summed, they must be multiplied by their respective prices and then summed up. Since prices are expressed in pounds, also national income and its components are expressed in pounds.

Even factor incomes – rents, interests, salaries, profits – which are part of national income, are real magnitudes, even if in modern economies they look like sums of money. From the example on clothes provided in the chapter devoted to Keynes we can clearly infer that such incomes exist even in a purely barter economy in which they are paid in kind and, being components of national income, they are quantities of commodities.

Sums of money, bonds and shares are instead *financial magnitudes* (and the quantity of money is a *monetary magnitude*), which do not exist in a barter economy. They are necessary to finance real magnitudes.

For instance, in order to make an investment (consisting in the purchase of machinery) a firm needs to find the funds to finance it, i.e. through which to buy the machinery. It may issue shares, bonds, or ask for a bank loan.[3]

Another example is given by public expenditure (which is a real magnitude). In order to carry out a certain expenditure (for example, to build a street or to increase public employees' wages), the government may collect funds in different ways: increasing taxes or issuing Treasury securities which are sold to the private sector, or issuing Treasury securities which are sold to the central bank. The size of the public expenditure (a real magnitude) is the same in all these three cases: but in the first one financial magnitudes do not change at all, in the second one the quantity of bonds in the economy increases, in the third one (*and only in this one*) the quantity of money increases.

Equipped by these instruments, we can compare the Keynesian

multiplier with the quantity theory of money. The multiplier analysis is based exclusively on real magnitudes. Actually, in that framework the level of national income depends only on investment and on the marginal propensity to consume. What matters is the size of investment, no matter how it is financed, either through the second method mentioned earlier (which does not imply the creation of new money), or through the third one, which implies a creation of money.[4] Therefore, a change in the quantity of money in circulation, *per se* does not affect the level of national income in any way.

This approach is poles apart the quantity theory according to which, as we have seen, an increase in the quantity of money, being immediately spent by individuals, determines an increase in aggregate demand and, consequently, an increase in prices if the economy is in full employment. Conversely, an increase in the quantity of money generates an expansion of output if there are unemployed resources.

As we have seen, according to Keynes, instead, the money introduced into the economy is not necessarily spent. Let us assume that the central bank increases the money supply through open market operations: i.e. it buys bonds from the private sector. By selling bonds to the central bank, individuals receive money in exchange, and they may deposit it at a bank. In this case, the process comes to a halt. In other words, individuals do not buy goods and services, but think that their income and wealth have remained unchanged since they exchanged bonds for money, and both represent two alternative ways of holding wealth. Therefore, neither an increase of the demand for goods nor an expansion of output occurs. Clearly, such a conclusion depends on Keynes' assumption that money is not only a medium of exchange, but also a store of value, i.e. a way to hold income and wealth.

Further, an increase in bank deposits, albeit raising the amount of loans banks *may* give to the firms, does not automatically lead to an increase of actual loans if firms have pessimistic expectations on the level of demand and profits and, accordingly, are not willing to expand investment.

These arguments have significant implications for economic policy. According to Keynes, when there is unemployment an expansion of aggregate demand is needed to eliminate it. A higher demand, in turn, can be obtained only through a higher volume of investment or an increase in the propensity to consume. On the other hand, demand is left untouched by an expansion of the money supply (pursued, for example, through open market operations), since it is not sure at all that such an expansion raises the volume of investments or the propensity to consume.

4.5 THE EFFECTS OF MONETARY POLICY ACCORDING TO KEYNES

The analysis of the two antithetical models relating to the Keynesian multiplier and the quantity theory of money enable us to address the following problem: are both the level of income (that is, of output) and the level of prices determined by real factors (like investment or the propensity to consume) or rather by monetary factors (the quantity of money in circulation)?

Actually Keynes himself, although emphasising the crucial role of real factors, acknowledged that changes in the quantity of money may affect the level of national income, but through a mechanism which differs from the one described by the quantity theory of money.

According to Keynes, changes in the quantity of money do not produce *direct* effects on the market of goods (as suggested by the quantity theory), but only on the market of bonds and, as we shall see, have *indirect* effects on that of goods.

If the central bank is willing to introduce money into the economy through open market operations it buys bonds and thus causes an increase in their prices. As we have seen, this lowers the interest rate (that is, the yield) of bonds. Then firms buy a lower quantity of bonds, that is they reduce their financial investment,[5] and expand real investment in raw materials (to be transformed into final products) and in machinery. Further, if the interest rate on bonds falls, banks will also reduce the interest rate they pay on customers' deposits.[6] Since for banks the cost of raising deposits falls, they will also reduce the interest rate for the firms to which they have granted credit (that is, the rate on loans). This makes firms increase their real investments. If there is unemployment, through the multiplier the increase in investment generates an expansion of both national income and employment.

An expansion of the money supply, then, determines an increase in investment. Such an increase, however, occurs through an *indirect* mechanism, which is not very effective.

According to Keynes, there are at least two reasons why, in the presence of unemployment, policies affecting real magnitudes (public investment, public consumption, tax reliefs, etc.) are surely more effective than monetary policies in reaching full employment. As we have seen, monetary policy affects investment only through the interest rate. Keynes argues that investment is affected only to a small extent by the interest rate since it depends mainly on firms' expectations on the level of demand (for the goods they produce) and on profits. If expectations are pessimistic, even a significant reduction in the interest rate (both on bonds and on the loans that banks grant to the firms) does not generate an increase in investment. Moreover, if the interest rate on bonds is at the lowest possible level (liquidity trap), it will not fall further. Hence, investment does not increase and monetary policy is completely ineffective.

An old controversy in the history of economic thought arises again: since the first decades of the last century the British economist D. Ricardo, having the long run in mind, reached the conclusion that the level of economic activity is determined only by real factors, while the quantity of money affects only the general level of prices. Instead, other economists (amongst them the British economist J. Stuart Mill), paying attention to the role of bank credit, suggested that in the short run monetary causes may have real effects and real causes may have monetary effects. This statement means that if, for example, real factors determine an expansion of the economy, the banking system tends to increase its loans to firms; on the other hand, if there is a financial panic, individuals withdraw their deposits from banks, which, in turn, reduce their loans to firms and, consequently, investment and other real magnitudes fall.

4.6 THE REDISCOVERY OF MONETARY POLICY AFTER THE SECOND WORLD WAR

After the Great Depression, the governments of the industrial countries implemented expansionary fiscal and monetary policies, and raised public expenditure, pushing the economy towards full employment. Money supply expansion caused a reduction in interest rates (also those on banks' loans to their customers), leading to what was termed *cheap money policy*. The outbreak of the Second World War raised aggregate demand speeding up the move towards full employment, since war needs augmented both public investment and public contracts for the private industry. Governments, therefore, had to finance such investment and contracts through an expansion of the public deficit, since taxation could not be raised over certain limits.

During the First World War governments followed the policy of issuing bonds at high interest rates in order to induce citizens to buy them. However, this was not enough to meet the enormous amount of war expenditure, and governments were obliged to print money, which made the price of goods soar.

During the Second World War Britain and the United States followed a different policy, partially suggested by Keynes in his short volume *How to pay for the war* (1940). Such a policy consisted essentially in restraining the consumption of households through rationing mechanisms which were effectively organised by the authorities and followed by the citizens. This forced individuals to save a high share of their income. The authorities prohibited the purchase of houses, jewels, and securities issued by firms which were not producing goods related to the military sector, and hence individuals were forced either to deposit their savings at a bank or to purchase bonds, which the government issued at *low interest rates*.

Since individuals could not invest in other forms, banks were able to offer extremely low interest rates on their deposits. Moreover, even banks were obliged to invest their deposits in government bonds, since it was not possible to purchase other assets. *Eventually, banks absorbed a very high share of public debt.*

Through these measures authorities partially restrained the expansion of aggregate demand and directed all the resources available towards war purposes, while curbing the public debt burden given the low interests paid to bondholders; in this way they also avoided creating money.

After the war, however, as the rationing of consumption ended, individuals demand for goods increased significantly and agents withdrew a large part of their bank deposits to pay for their purchases. On the other hand, in order to satisfy the high demand, firms had to convert their plant to produce commodities other than those related to war, and they needed funds to make such a conversion; therefore, they

46

asked the banks for credit. In order to give households and firms money, banks had to sell a very large part of the bonds they held.

The central bank thus had to choose between alternative options. It could purchase government bonds (through open market operations): this would have halted the fall in the price of bonds (and the increase in the interest rate), but at the same time it would have introduced new money into the economy. At first, the monetary authorities adopted this policy, fearing that the sale of bonds on behalf of banks (that is, their *monetisation*) would lead to a confidence crisis in the bond market and hence a panic on financial markets with a consequent crisis of confidence of savers who would not purchase bonds any longer. Later on, however, the central bank abandoned the policy of sustaining the prices of bonds, that is it did not purchase securities any longer, and allowed their prices to be determined by the market. In this way the central bank ceased raising the money supply, which increased inflationary impulses due to the significant expansion of the demand for goods.

The feared panic on financial markets failed to occur since, once banks started selling bonds, their prices started falling. As some economists and in particular R. Roosa had foreseen, such a fall, although not significant, was big enough to halt the sale of bonds from the banks, since it determined serious capital losses. Obviously, once they reduced bond sales, banks faced a shortage of cash and hence curtailed their loans to firms. Therefore, they reduced credit not by raising the interest rate on loans[7] but rather by rationing credit, that is discriminating according to their customers importance and to their creditworthiness.

The expansion of the money supply was thus halted, which was exactly the objective the authorities wanted to achieve. Since the support of security prices was abandoned in the Anglo-Saxon countries starting in 1951, the latter was regarded as the year in which the 'rediscovery of monetary policy' occurred. Actually, Keynesian analysis had led to an undervaluation of the role of monetary policy; in the Thirties and Fourties governments had followed expansionary monetary policies; in the Fifties for the first time after some twenty years, authorities returned temporarily to a restrictive monetary policy. This proved that by then the industrial world had definitively recovered from the Great Depression and once the war – in which military requirements had led to full employment – was over, the aggregate demand (personal consumption and firms' investment) remained high. In these circumstances not only there was no danger of a new depression, but governments were called to adopt measures to restrict demand, that is the opposite of the ones suggested by Keynes during the Thirties.

4.7 THE ECONOMY'S OVERALL LIQUIDITY AND ITS REGULATION

The events described in the previous paragraph show that during the Fifties financial markets were closely linked to the amount of public sector debt, its distribution among economic agents and monetary policy. From the empirical evidence of such phenomena, during the Fifties several economists assessed that economic analysis cannot consider simply the effects of changes in the quantity of money on real magnitudes (investment, national income, etc.), but it must also take into account the existence of financial activities other than money (in particular public debt bonds), whose volume and distribution among subjects may affect real magnitudes just like money.

When we talk about money we usually refer to cash. In this respect, one must consider that money which is held by the public is only *potentially* subject to multiplication: it is multiplied only if it is deposited at a bank. Cash deposited at banks, instead, is subject to the multiplicative process described earlier. Since the deposits appearing in the statistics have already been subject to the multiplicative process, we generally consider money to be equivalent to cash held by the public plus bank deposits. A more detailed analysis has led us earlier (see paragraph 4.2) to regard the monetary base, rather than cash, as the magnitude subject to multiplication.

At the end of the Fifties, the *Radcliffe Report* on the working of the British monetary system (produced by several economists) maintained that it is not sufficient to consider the quantity of money or the monetary base, but it is necessary to look at the *structure of the liquidity* in the economy, since it is the latter which affects investment and income.

How can the structure of liquidity be defined? First of all we need to consider that, besides banks, there are several institutions which, like the former, collect savings from the public and finance firms or other agents. *Financial intermediaries other than banks* are very diffuse in

England and in the United States. These are insurance companies, institutions for hire-purchase, building societies, pension funds, etc.

As two American economists, Gurley and Shaw, have pointed out, such institutions collect money by issuing securities and create differentiated securities according to savers' needs, that is according to the risk the latter are willing to undertake (for example, securities which are intermediate between bonds and shares may yield a certain minimum income and an uncertain additional income: they can be closer to bonds or to shares), and according to duration (securities can be reimbursed after a few days or many months or years). Further, such institutions may even grant loans, adapting them to the different firms, diversifying them in their duration, requirements of guarantee, etc. Finally, they often own significant quantities of public debt bonds, which they may decide to sell (that is, to monetise) or to keep, with the consequences described in the previous paragraph.

The existence of financial non-banking intermediaries raises delicate problems of monetary policy. Monetary authorities cannot limit themselves to control the quantity of money (or the monetary base) and banks' behaviour. In order to affect investment and aggregate demand, they have to control the behaviour of financial intermediators as well. If the latter have a high liquidity (that is, money), they could grant loans to firms even when the central bank pursues a restrictive monetary policy (for example, it reduces anticipations or the rediscount of bills to commercial banks). In this way, therefore, the effects of the central bank's monetary policy are distorted or reduced. Since the relations between the central bank and non-banking financial intermediaries do not in general coincide with those occurring between the central bank and commercial banks (anticipations, rediscount, compulsory reserve), new forms of administrative control for non-banking intermediaries must be found. Obviously, in order to give more precise prescriptions, we need to refer to the particular institutions present in each state.

In Anglo-Saxon countries there is a large number of non-banking financial intermediaries which operate in a very specialised way, creating a big variety of securities, each differing for risk and duration. Even public debt bonds differ in their duration: there are securities maturing after a few days or months and others maturing after years. The former are very similar to money, and for this reason some economists call them *near money*, since they could be used also to make payments.

49

In general, the closer the maturity the more liquid the security is. Then, monetary authorities need to control not only the quantity of money and the monetary base but also the amount of near money and, in general, the *liquidity structure of the economy*.

When monetary authorities decide to raise liquidity, they have to purchase long term securities and sell short term ones. If the total amount of bonds remains unchanged, money is neither reduced nor raised, but the *maturity structure* of the amount of fixed yield securities changes, since the quantity of the least liquid bonds falls and that of the most liquid ones increases. When the central bank purchases long term securities, this causes an increase in their price and a fall in their yield rate, i.e. the long term interest rate; when the central bank sells short term securities, this makes their price fall and the short term interest rate rise. The authorities have to do the opposite when they want to reduce the economy's liquidity.

The previous considerations illustrate extensively the notion of 'general liquidity of the economy' and the problem of its control. We can add some further considerations.

Even a shop keeper that grants credit to a customer for his daily shopping, allowing him to settle his payments once a month, creates liquidity. In the same way, a firm selling goods to another firm creates liquidity when it allows delayed payment. In both instances the liquidity created is a form of *trade credit*.

Finally, hire-purchase finance deserves particular attention. This is a method which is largely used, other than for investment goods, for durable consumption goods, like cars, electrical household appliances, etc. In Britain and the United States hire-purchase finance is managed by special institutions, traditionally owned by banks in the UK, but also by other institutions.

An agent paying for a good with instalments signs some bills which the seller discounts through the banking system. The quantity of bills the banking system discounts determines the amount of instalment credit available in the economy. Moreover, the interests buyers have to pay sellers depends upon the level of the discount rate on bills (which sellers have to pay the bank). An increase in the amount of instalment credit available or a decrease in the discount rate may, therefore, cause an increase in instalment contracts. Since these are essentially related to consumption goods, an increase in the propensity to consume occurs and hence also in national income. It is important to notice that this type of monetary manoeuvre affects the propensity to consume rather than investment.

4.8 A DISCUSSION OF THE THEORETICAL BASES OF KEYNESIAN ECONOMICS AND THE PROBLEM OF THE NEUTRALITY OF MONEY

Keynes showed that the economy has no mechanism capable of achieving full employment automatically. This is because, first of all, wages are not flexible downwards. However, according to Keynes, even if wages were flexible, in the presence of unemployed workers a fall in wages would reduce the demand for consumption goods and hence firms' production; therefore, rather than increasing, employment would be further reduced.

Several economists have attempted to deny this argument, trying to show that an automatic mechanism leading to full employment exists. Pigou, in particular, stated that a reduction in wages, determining a reduction in aggregate demand as Keynes maintained, would cause a fall in the price of goods and this would lead to an increase in the real value of the monetary balances (that is, money) owned by individuals (the so called *Pigou effect* or *real balance effect*). Obviously, if prices fall, people can buy a larger amount of goods with a given sum of money. Individuals, then, feel richer and accordingly increase their demand for consumption goods. This raises output, pushing the economy towards full employment.[8]

In this way Pigou maintained that price flexibility guarantees full employment, even if he admitted that such a downward flexibility actually does not exist in modern economies, also because this mechanism would require a big fall of prices to achieve full employment.

Patinkin used Pigou's analysis to deepen the investigation on the effects of a change of monetary magnitudes on real variables in the automatic readjustment mechanism.

At this point we need to introduce the concept of the *neutrality of money*. Money is neutral when variations in its quantity do not affect the real magnitudes of the economy. In Fisher's theory, money is neutral since changes in its quantity affect only the absolute level of prices, but not investment or the national income in real terms (that is, the physical quantities produced) or the relative prices of goods.[9] Therefore, in the quantity theory the neutrality of money leads to a separation (or *dichotomy*) of monetary and real phenomena. Money is a *veil* which does not affect real magnitudes.

In Keynesian theory money is not neutral. As we have seen, changes in its quantity determine changes in the interest rate, and hence in the price of bonds. Since the prices of goods remain unchanged while those of securities change, a variation in the relative prices between goods and securities occurs. Further, changes in the interest rate affect, even if only to a small extent, investment and consequently national income. Therefore, changes in the quantity of money influence the real magnitudes.

Using the Pigou effect, Patinkin shows that, if a fall in prices makes individuals feel richer due to the appreciation of their money balances, they will expand consumption. Hence, the demand for goods increases. Prices thus rise and the economy returns to equilibrium, that is to the situation experienced before the fall in prices. Hence, through the Pigou effect, money turns out to be neutral since eventually it does not affect the level of national income and employment (neither the relative prices if we neglect the effects of a change in the quantity of money on the interest rate). However, in this context the neutrality of money does not imply a dichotomy in the economy, given that monetary phenomena (which are dependent upon the real value of money stocks owned by individuals) affect the demand for goods, i.e. a real magnitude.

Patinkin's analysis has been developed by several economists, through the use of complex mathematical instruments. Patinkin himself, however, recognises the limited empirical content of the Pigou effect; hence, in practice, Keynes' conclusions concerning the fact that the economy is likely to stagnate in an underemployment equilibrium remain valid.

In the debate concerning the Pigou effect, several authors stressed the relevance of both creditors' and debtors' behaviour in the economy. A generalised decrease in prices makes creditors feel richer since the real value of their credit augments (with the amount of money they receive, creditors can purchase a larger quantity of goods), while for the same reasons debtors feel poorer. Therefore, a decrease of prices leads creditors to consume more and debtors to consume less; consequently the aggregate demand for goods does not change. Rather, if the psychological effect of the debtors impoverishment is larger than the psychological effect of creditors enrichment, the result could be an overall reduction in consumption. These considerations were formulated by I. Fisher even before the publication of Keynes' *General Theory*. However, the Pigouvian effect, related to both monetary stocks and public debt securities, remains. The private sector which owns monetary stocks is a creditor of the central bank (which issues money); those who hold government securities are creditors of the Treasury. A reduction in the price of goods, by augmenting the real value of both monetary stocks and securities, makes the owners of these assets consume more, while obviously it does not produce any effect on the behaviour of both the central bank and the Treasury.

In this respect the distinction between *outside money* and *inside money* introduced by Gurley and Shaw in the Fifties and Sixties returns. If money is created by an authority provided with such a power (the central bank), which uses its power to buy goods and services from the private sector, then this is outside money. By financing the Treasury's deficit, the central bank allows the Treasury to buy goods and services from the private sector (for example, the Treasury may carry out public investments or may raise civil servants' wages). In this case money is outside the private sector and represents a net financial asset for the latter. However, money can be created also within the private sector (inside money): this occurs when banks collect deposits from their customers and lend money to firms. In this case the people depositing their money are creditors and the borrowing firms are debtors. As we have seen, inside money is created also by financial intermediators different from banks and even by firms allowing other firms and agents to delay payments.

4.9 MONETARISM

While the *Radcliffe Report* rediscovered the importance of monetary policy and maintained that the latter must not be limited to a mere consideration of the money supply but must be extended to an analysis of the liquidity structure of the whole economy, Milton Friedman and other economists of the Chicago School (the so called *monetarists*) considered the effects of money supply on real magnitudes, arguing that the quantity of money is the most important aggregate in the economy.

As we have already seen, Friedman made an important contribution to the theory of the demand for money, developing the Keynesian idea that money is one of the forms in which agents hold wealth. Like Tobin and other authors, Friedman introduces the theory of the demand for money in the analysis of portfolio choices, that is in agents' decisions of how to distribute wealth among different assets.

Moreover, by means of empirical research, Friedman investigated the effects of changes in the money supply on the real variables of the economy (particularly on national income) and on the level of prices, reaching the conclusion that an excessive increase in the money supply causes an increase in prices, while a reduction produces a decrease of both investment and income since in modern economies prices are sticky downwards.

Therefore, the conclusion that Friedman reached on this point is different from that of Keynes and quite similar to that of the quantity theory. From these considerations Friedman draws relevant conclusions concerning the implementation of monetary policy. Several Keynesian economists suggested to use monetary policy as a stabilising measure, expanding money supply during the periods of crisis to stimulate investment and national income, and reducing it during inflation to curtail aggregate demand and thus restrain the price rise. Friedman rejects the argument and argues that changes in the quantity of money produce effects on real magnitudes with a sensible *lag*. Therefore, monetary policy would produce an expansionary effect on investment when the economy is overcoming the crisis automatically; this would raise aggregate demand too much, with a consequent increase of prices if the economy is not far from full employment.

In a similar way, the restraining effects of monetary policy would come into effect when expansion, with its inflationary impulses, is vanishing and they would create a depression. These considerations are based on the belief, opposite to that of Keynes, that the economy has an automatic self-regulating capacity, and it tends to overcome any crisis and inflation without external intervention.

Consequently, Friedman argues that monetary policy cannot keep the interest rate at a predetermined level. According to Friedman, the cheap money policy pursued during and after the Second World War shows the failure of such an attempt. Actually, in order to maintain a low interest rate, monetary authorities were forced to introduce larger and larger amounts of money into the economy (they bought securities, keeping their price high and therefore the interest rate low). This raised the availability of money for both individuals and banks which, in turn, increased the amount of loans available for the firms. A large part of the demand for goods and services was financed in this way, and the expansion of demand with respect to a supply that was growing slowly generated an increase in prices.

In other words, Friedman suggests that an expansion in the quantity of money, sooner or later, affects the goods market, generating inflation. The price rise makes agents find the interest rates on bonds too low, and thus they reduce their purchases of bonds. Therefore, monetary authorities are forced to buy larger and larger quantities of bonds in order to sustain their prices and to keep the interest rate low. However, in this way they worsen the inflationary process and are consequently forced to reduce the creation of new money, that is the purchase of bonds. This was what actually happened; the price of bonds declined and the interest rate rose.

In a similar way, if the economy faces unemployment (for example, of four or five per cent of the total labour force), this cannot be eliminated only through the use of an expansionary monetary policy. Such a policy would temporarily raise investment and hence absorb unemployment. However, introducing money into the economy when unemployment is not particularly high makes aggregate demand stimulate aggregate supply (which in a situation of almost full employment may increase only by a small extent) and consequently prices rise. If trade unions do not take account of nominal wages (the amount of money the average worker is paid) but rather of real wages (the purchasing power of this amount), they ask for – and obtain – further rises of nominal wages. If the latter represents an excessive burden for firms, unemployment appears again. Authorities are again forced to raise the money supply and the inflationary process becomes stronger and stronger. Monetary policy therefore is not able to achieve full employment if trade unions ask for a *real* wage that is higher than that of equilibrium, i.e. that absorbing unemployment completely and making (workers) labour supply equal to (entrepreneurs) labour demand. In other words, unemployment results from the monopoly power of trade unions.

The conclusion reached by Friedman is that, in general, policies aimed at achieving stability in the economy generate instability, while stability may be achieved only through the free operation of market forces. Then, while Keynes and his followers emphasised the intrinsic instability of an advanced capitalist economy and maintained the necessity of a continuous state intervention to manage the level of aggregate demand both through monetary policy and, more important still, through fiscal policy (that is, public expenditure and taxation), for monetarists the private sector is essentially stable and its main instabilities stem from the intervention of the authorities. Therefore, the latter must not expand money supply in periods of crisis and reduce it during inflation, but rather they should expand money supply at a constant rate of about three or four per cent a year, nearly equal to that of the expansion of national income. The market forces themselves (both relating to demand and to supply) correct the recessive and inflationary tendencies which arise during the economy's growth.

The adoption of a regular and stable behaviour on behalf of the authorities generates a stable environment for both consumers and firms and thus avoids crises and 'excessively high' inflation. Friedman's perspective implies, then, the adoption of *automatic rules* on behalf of authorities rather than *discretionary rules*, as the Keynesian school suggests.

Friedman's conclusions would not have had unanimous consent even in the past century, when several economists (for example J.S. Mill) considered the banking system intrinsically unstable (for instance, a panic situation could arise, individuals would withdraw their deposits from banks fearing that these may become insolvent, banks would reduce their loans to firms, firms could go bankrupt and lay off workers, hence both unemployment and a reduction of investment would occur). Therefore, these economists thought that the banking system requires careful management on behalf of the central bank, based on discretionary judgements, rather than on the adoption of mechanical rules.

NOTES

1. The bank gives the individual a lower amount than that promised in the bill since it is allowed to collect his credit only after a while, i.e. when the bill matures. The discount, then, is the inverse operation of the calculation of the interest on a bank deposit.

This statement may be further analysed through an example. If today I deposit one pound in a bank and the interest rate is ten per cent, after one year I will get 1.10 pounds. Consider the opposite operation: if I have a credit of 1.10 collectable after a year, this is equivalent to one pound today. In fact, if the debtor paid me one pound today, I could deposit it in a bank and after one year I would have 1.10 pounds. Therefore, if the interest rate on deposits is 10 per cent, 1.10 pounds after one year are equal to one pound today.

2. On these points see also chapter eleven.

3. Also the purchase of shares and bonds on behalf of a firm or the private sector is generally called investment. This is, however, a *financial investment*, while the purchase of raw materials, machinery, buildings (that is the purchase of investment goods) are *real investments*. Naturally, it is real investment that is included in the national product.

4. In a Keynesian framework, instead, financing public investment through money raised by new taxes has a disadvantage: it reduces agents' *disposable income* (that is, the income they can actually spend) and, accordingly, consumption. In this way the marginal propensity to consume falls which, in turn, reduces the expansive effect due to public investment.

5. When bonds provide high yields, many firms prefer to buy them rather than raw materials and machinery that allow to expand output.

6. If we consider the (realistic) hypothesis that deposit accounts yield an interest, this will be lower than the interest rate on bonds, otherwise individuals would prefer to hold money in bank deposits rather than to invest it in bonds. Then, a reduction in the interest rate on bonds induces banks to reduce the rate on deposits, since individuals continue to deposit money in banks notwithstanding the reduction.

7. Actually, as the fall in securities' prices slowed down so did the rise of the interest rate on securities, and, accordingly, also that of other interest rates (on deposits and on loans). For a discussion on the links between different interest rates, see the previous paragraph.

8. Pigou emphasised that an individual's consumption depends not only on his income but also on his wealth; several economists, like Modigliani and others, have shown the importance of this argument.

9. The difference between the absolute level of prices and relative prices may be illustrated through a simple example. Let us suppose that the price of one pound of apples is one sterling and that the price of one pound of pears is three sterling. The relative price of apples is ⅓ (actually, the price of one pound of apples is equal to ⅓ of one pound of pears) and the relative price of pears is

$$\frac{3}{1} = 3$$

Let us suppose, now, that the quantity of money in circulation doubles. The absolute level of prices doubles: the price of one pound of apples will be two sterling and the price of one pound of pears six sterling. Relative prices do not change. Actually

$$\frac{1}{3} = \frac{2}{6} \text{ and } \frac{3}{1} = \frac{6}{2}$$

Relative prices are a real magnitude since they exist also in a barter economy and can be expressed without money. For example, if two pigs are needed to buy one sheep, this means that the price of one sheep is two pigs and the price of one pig is 1/2 sheep. Instead, the absolute level of prices can be expressed only through money and it is a monetary magnitude. In the last example, an infinite number of absolute levels of prices may correspond to given relative prices. It is sufficient to attribute any given price in sterling to one pig and the price of one pig will always be double than that of one sheep.

5 Fiscal and monetary policies and economic stability

5.1 NEO-KEYNESIAN THEORY AND THE COMBINED USE OF MONETARY AND FISCAL POLICY

At the beginning of the Sixties, the economic advisers of the President of the United States reconsidered the Keynesian concept of potential income providing it with a more operational definition. In industrial societies, such as the United States, individuals often change their job and, in passing from one job to another, they remain unemployed for some time. Moreover sometimes women leave work when they are pregnant or have young children and return to work later on. Therefore, an economy always has a certain level of unemployment due to these – and other similar – reasons, which is called *frictional unemployment*. The latter amounts to three or four per cent of the total labour force (that is, of people in working age). *Potential income*, then, is defined as the national income produced by the economy when the amount of unemployment is about three or four per cent, i.e. when employment is at its highest possible level.

The economic advisers of the White House argued that at the beginning of the Sixties unemployment in the United States amounted to about seven per cent; further, plant and machinery was utilised at eighty per cent and, therefore, the system was underutilising its potential resources. Hence, an expansionary economic policy was needed, until actual production reached potential production. The *gap*, i.e. the difference between the two would have been filled only when unemployment reached three or four per cent of the labour force. This innovation with respect to Keynes consisted in refining the instruments (including statistical ones) to calculate potential income.

In order to fill the gap between actual and potential output, neo-Keynesian economists suggested introducing fiscal policies, both in the form of a tax reduction and an increase in public expenditure, to be financed through a budget deficit (i.e. through an issue of public debt bonds), following Keynes' teaching.

The implementation of these policies during the Sixties led the American economy to operate close to full employment; however, some inflationary pressure started appearing in the economy. A price rise not only produces domestic negative effects, as we shall see in the next chapter on inflation, but it also creates difficulties for the balance of payments given that, if the exchange rates among currencies are fixed – as they were during the Sixties – it makes exports less competitive on international markets, determining their reduction, whilst it causes an increase in imports which become cheaper than domestic goods.[1] It is necessary, therefore, to contain the expansion of aggregate demand. Experience however shows that fiscal policy may be followed more easily in an expansionary direction than in a restrictive one: from a political point of view, it is often difficult to increase taxation or to reduce public expenditure at the right time. The idea thus emerged that there is an inconsistency between full employment on one side (*domestic equilibrium*) and both price stability and balance of payments equilibrium on the other side (*external equilibrium*).

Several economists, then, have observed that, since short run economic policy must pursue two goals simultaneously – domestic and external equilibrium – one instrument (fiscal policy) is not enough to pursue both goals, but it is necessary to combine two instruments: fiscal and monetary policy. As we have seen, the former may be more easily implemented in an expansionary direction rather than in a restrictive one, while the latter is more effective in a restrictive rather than in an expansionary direction.[2] Therefore, some economists have suggested to adopt expansionary fiscal policies mainly to reach full employment (that is, domestic equilibrium) and to combine them with a cautious (even if not decidedly restrictive) monetary policy, in order to keep the price dynamics under control. This tends to restore balance of payments equilibrium (external equilibrium). Moreover, a restrictive monetary policy (for example pursued through the central bank's sale of public debt bonds), which raises the interest rate on bonds by reducing their prices, also makes foreign investors purchase bonds. Hence, an inflow of foreign currency, which enhances the balance of payments.

From the Seventies on a floating exchange rate system was introduced, which made the manipulation of the exchange rate become another feasible economic policy instrument. On the basis of such a consideration and keeping in mind the problems faced by the British economy, the economists of the New Cambridge School (England) suggested to assign to a restrictive fiscal policy, i.e. to a reduction of the public sector deficit, the task of restoring balance of payments equilibrium in the medium period. On the other hand, they suggest assigning the task of stimulating economic activity to a devaluation of the exchange rate. We shall come back to this topic in chapter eleven.

5.2 THE INCREASING ROLE OF THE STATE IN THE ECONOMY AND ITS EFFECTS ON THE PUBLIC BUDGET; ORIGIN AND CRISIS OF THE WELFARE STATE

After the Second World War, the governments of the main industrial countries raised not only public investment (as Keynes had suggested, to eliminate unemployment) but also current expenditure (wages and salaries of public employees, pensions, etc.). Actually, a 'welfare state' ideology emerged, according to which the state should guarantee all citizens some social services free of charge (compulsory education, at least until a certain age, and medical care), some goods and services at a low price (housing, public transport, etc.), pensions, unemployment subsidies, etc. In order to guarantee these services, the state had to hire a large number of people (teachers, doctors, nurses, etc.) and hence it raised public expenditure for wages, salaries and pensions, that is current expenditure.

Both in the Keynesian period (the Thirties) and in the post-Keynesian period (the years after the Second World War), governments faced the problem of how to finance (i.e. how to get the money to pay for) such expenses. This is possible by three different ways: governments may increase taxation; they may issue public debt bonds and thus borrow money from citizens (deficit spending); they may create money.

Keynes underlined that during the Thirties industrial economies were affected by a lack of demand (families and firms did not buy enough goods); therefore he maintained that it was necessary to stimulate demand, by hiring unemployed people and giving them a salary. According to Keynes, if governments increased taxation, disposable income would fall; accordingly, consumers would reduce consumption. In conclusion, Keynes argued that the state should find the money to carry out public investment (and thus to engage unemployed people and pay them a salary) not by raising taxation, but rather by issuing public debt bonds. This policy was called deficit spending, given that it meant financing expenditure through a budget deficit.

During the post-war period the situation was different. After the Second World War, in the main industrial countries demand for goods was high and unemployment was low. Governments raised current expenditure enormously (for salaries and pensions) and hence they had to finance it also by augmenting taxation. In all industrial countries both the ratio of public expenditure to gross national product and the tax to GNP ratio rose. Taxes grew more rapidly than GNP. Since GNP is wealth (i.e. the sum of all goods and services) produced in a country in one year, this means that the state, through taxation, levied increasing shares of wealth produced by the private sector. The rise in the tax to GNP ratio was pursued by making taxation more progressive.

The rise in the tax to GNP ratio, however, was not sufficient to cover the huge expansion of public expenditure that occurred in industrial countries, especially from the Sixties on. Such an expansion was essentially due to social expenditure imposed by the ideology of the welfare state, but in some countries, like in the United States, it was also due to the increased military expenditure.

Moreover, during the Seventies a proper *antitax revolt* occurred in many countries. This took place in Sweden, Britain and the United States; governments were forced to reduce the progressiveness of taxation. For example, in some countries (Sweden, Britain, etc.), the highest tax rate exceeded ninety per cent. The antitax revolt occurred both through citizens trying to escape taxation by semi-legal ways, and through the ballot box. Actually, during the Seventies, in both Scandinavian countries and Britain, and eventually the United States, elections were won by conservative parties which promised, and partially carried out, a tax reduction and a curb in progressiveness. Both Mrs. Thatcher in Britain and Reagan in the United States reduced the tax burden.

Therefore, during the Seventies and Eighties, governments could not raise the tax to GNP ratio; conversely, in some countries they were forced to reduce it. Some governments attempted to cut down public expenditure, but they succeeded only to a small extent. Therefore, during the Seventies and Eighties many industrial countries experienced continuous increases in the public sector deficit. Governments faced the problem of financing the public deficit either by issuing public debt bonds or money.

Let us consider how in practice these two forms of financing occur. Public debt bonds are issued by the Treasury, i.e. by the government; money, instead, is created by the central bank. The central bank enjoys a certain autonomy from the government; this is true for all countries, even if this varies from country to country. If the Treasury sells its bonds to the private sector, there is an increase in the public debt, but no creation of new money. However, the private sector is not always willing to purchase Treasury bonds. In particular, in order to make the private sector purchase them, the yield (i.e. the interest rate) of bonds must rise. In this way, however, the Treasury has to pay higher interest, and hence bears new expenses. Actually, it is unthinkable that in peacetime a government may adopt measures similar to those adopted by British and American authorities during the Second World War, in order to finance the war, keeping interest rates low. In order to avoid a rise in interest rates, the Treasury could ask the central bank to buy the bonds; the central bank (which enjoys a certain autonomy, but is in practice always subordinate to the government) could purchase them, even if they yield a low interest rate. In this case the central bank gives the Treasury money and hence money creation occurs. This solution is less costly for the Treasury, which pays a lower amount in interest, but determines an increase in the quantity of money in circulation, and hence inflation.

Technically, a government may either encourage a 'divorce' of the central bank from the Treasury or a 'marriage' between the two. In the first case, the Treasury issues public debt bonds at a given interest rate. If the private sector purchases only part of them, the central bank is not bound to buy all the unsold bonds. Therefore, if the Treasury needs money, it must try to sell its bonds to the private sector, and hence it is obliged to raise the interest rates. In this way public debt increases, but there is no money creation. The public deficit is financed through the market.

In the case of a 'marriage' between the central bank and the Treasury, the latter issues public debt bonds at a given interest rate. If the private sector purchases only a part of these bonds, the central bank is bound to buy all the unsold ones. A deficit is then financed through money creation. 'Marriage' allows the Treasury to keep the interest rate on bonds low, but it implies money creation, thus generating inflation.

'Divorce' between the central bank and the Treasury avoids financing deficits through money creation and hence inflation,[3] but it increases the interest rate on public debt bonds. This has two negative effects: an increase in the state's interest bill and a reduction of private firms investment. Actually, when the state offers high yields on public debt bonds, savers do not deposit their money in a bank, but rather they buy bonds. Banks, then, have low deposits and hence a small amount of money to lend to firms. In order to collect money, banks have to raise the interest rates they pay on their customers deposits, thus inducing savers to deposit at least part of their bank savings. However, since banks have to pay higher interest rates on their customers deposits, they have to raise the interest rates on the loans they grant firms. Therefore, since firms have to pay banks higher interest rates, they borrow less, and consequently they reduce the purchases of plant, machinery, etc. needed to expand their activity.

In other words, the increase of public expenditure financed through a public debt increase reduces, i.e. crowds out, private expenditure. This phenomenon is named *crowding out*.

To avoid these inconveniences, sometimes governments have preferred the 'marriage' regime. This, however, raises the quantity of money and hence inflation.

In recent years, in some countries (for example, in Britain) governments have attempted, with some success, to reduce public expenditure, making citizens pay, at least in part, for their education, health services, etc. Several countries (Britain, the United States, Italy, Sweden, etc.) have also made taxation less progressive. Therefore a partial inversion of the trend with respect to the welfare state ideology has occurred.

5.3 CROWDING OUT, SOCIAL CONFLICTS AND INFLATION, SUPPLY SIDE ECONOMICS

The events just described led economists to reconsider Keynes' contribution, according to which public expenditure financed through deficit does not crowd out private expenditure, nor does it create inflation. The hypothesis on which Keynesian theory rests is that unemployed people and unused machinery are present in the economy and therefore output can be expanded (that is supply is elastic) until the full employment barrier is met. In this case public expenditure (in particular public investment) financed through deficits adds to, and does not substitute itself to, private expenditure, and hence it raises income and employment through the multiplicative process.

Some authors have insisted on the existence of crowding-out. According to this theory public expenditure crowds out private expenditure and, being the latter's productivity higher than that of the former, the growth rate of the economy falls.

Other economists, instead, focused on the inflationary effects that public expenditure may produce. The high public deficits and the high inflation rates experienced by most industrial countries during the Seventies led many economists to reconsider Keynesian theory. Some of them resurrected, in a modern perspective, the bulk of free market doctrines, that, beyond a certain limit, public expenditure is unproductive. Both public expenditure on welfare and a progressive tax system, which represent the core of the welfare state, raise agents risk-aversiveness and hence reduce the growth rate of investment and output. When supply is not very elastic, an expansion of demand produces inflation and/or a deficit in the balance of payments. Several authors of the continental school, from Einaudi to Röpke, have always supported these ideas, even when Keynesian theory was very trendy.

According to their point of view, the cause of inflation is the volume of public expenditure (with respect to national income) rather than the deficit. Some of these economists stressed the negative psychological effects that the size of the government budget produces on economic agents. However, the central idea underlying this theory is that the public sector does not operate according to market rules. Other economists, however, argued that this approach represents an ideological position rather than a proper theory.

Two recent versions of this theory, developed in a more modern perspective, are the *tax induced* or *social conflict-induced inflation theory* and *supply side economics*.

The tax induced inflation, put forward by some British, Italian and Scandinavian economists, rests on the experience of these countries and may be summarised as follows. An expansion of public expenditure pushes the authorities to raise the tax to GNP ratio as well as tax progressiveness. Agents who have to bear the burden of the increase attempt to transfer it to other subjects. This generates inflation. The inflationary process is the outcome of a conflict concerning income distribution, that is a social conflict. In particular, price makers (firms, traders, etc.), being hit by taxation, raise the prices of the commodities and services they sell. Employees, who earn fixed salaries and are price takers, react by raising social conflicts and asking for a wage increase; in this way the inflationary process is self-feeding. This happens also because workers with fixed wages are guaranteed by salary indexation mechanisms (that make wages automatically rise with prices).

One main point of this theory, however, remains open: if monetary policy is not expansionary, i.e. if it does not fuel the price rise, are the tax burden transfer and an inflationary process feasible?

It is at this point that the contrast between Keynesians and monetarists arises.

It is obvious that an inflationary process may be self-feeding and persist in the long run only if there is an adequate expansion of the money supply. The limit within which inflationary impulses may produce price rises when the quantity of money does not grow is essentially an empirical issue, which econometric investigation can prove only on a case-by-case basis.

The other modern version of the free market perspective is the supply side economics. According to this approach, the only way to accelerate the growth of the economy is to provide an incentive to private investment, which will raise productive capacity, that is supply. To reach this goal, it is necessary to reduce public expenditure, taxation and the regulation of private activities. The underlying idea is that these three elements (public expenditure, taxation and regulation) distort market mechanisms and reduce investment, productivity and growth. In such a situation policies aimed at stimulating demand produce only inflation.

Actually, the exponents of the supply side economics argue that the excessive increases in taxation make individuals work less, that is produce less, as they have to surrender a large proportion of their earnings to the state. Moreover, the increase of pensions, the supply of free health services and education, the high subsidies in favour of the unemployed make individuals work and save less. Finally, the excessive regulation of private economic activity (urban and regional planning, environmental policy, policies regulating the working environment, etc.) represents an obstacle to investment and production.

During the Eighties the Reagan Administration in the United States claimed it wanted to pursue an economic policy inspired by such principles, but it was unable to reduce public expenditure. Actually it raised military expenditure without reducing social expenditure. The public deficit, far from falling, actually rose. But at least in a first stage, authorities financed the deficit through the market rather than through money creation. The outcome was a significant increase in interest rates. This leads us to explore the effects that different ways of financing public deficits may have on economic variables.

An important point of view concerning the relationship between public deficit and inflation is the monetarist one. They argue that budget deficits and changes in fiscal policy have only limited effects on the level of economic activity and on prices, unless they are accompanied by variations in the money stock. The exponents of the so called *fiscal monetarism* maintain that the enormous expansion of the public deficit that occurred in the last few years in most industrial countries led governments to raise money supply, and this generated inflation. However, the policy endorsed in several countries envisaging a 'divorce' between the central bank and the Treasury shows that no automatic relationship between the growth of the deficit and money creation exists. The fundamental feature of monetarists is that they regard money as a special asset, totally different from other financial assets.

Several authors have analysed the different forms of deficit financing and their impact on the level of economic activity and prices. There is a wide range of results, ranging from one stating that only money matters in determining the level of economic activity and therefore of inflation, to one, which argues that money matters but other components of wealth are relevant too, to yet another one which states that financing by public debt is more inflationary than monetary financing. Many of these models are too simplified and hence they cannot be verified empirically. Also many econometric models, relating to different countries, have been produced, but in general they do not give clear cut results.

5.4 RATIONAL EXPECTATIONS THEORY AND THE NEW CLASSICAL MACROECONOMICS; THE DEBATE ON THE STABILITY OF THE ECONOMY

Keynes emphasised how the decisions of economic agents are taken in a condition of uncertainty concerning the future behaviour of the economy. A firm which must decide whether or not to undertake an investment (for instance, to build or to purchase a plant that produces certain goods) tries to forecast the future demand for these goods, the possible development of technology in the sector, production costs, etc. Economic agents, and firms in particular, make forecasts and therefore form expectations about the future behaviour of the economy. The problem of how expectations are formed has been examined by many economists and represents one of the most controversial topics in economic theory.

The most simple hypothesis is that agents predict that in the following period economic variables (prices, wages, production, etc.) will have the same values as today (*static expectations*). An alternative assumption is that, if prices grow at a certain rate (for example, four per cent) during a given year, in the following year they will grow at the same rate (*extrapolative expectations*). A more sophisticated version is the hypothesis of *adaptive expectations*, according to which the forecast value of an economic variable is influenced not only by the recent values of the variable, but also by its values in the more distant past.

More recently, some economists have developed the theory of *rational expectations*, which has been utilised particularly by the so called *new classical macroeconomics.*

According to the rational expectations hypothesis, in forecasting the trend of the economy, economic agents (mainly big firms) behave rationally, that is, they use all the available information, including information about the past condition of the economy and the past behaviour of the authorities that manage economic policy (fiscal and monetary). Naturally, agents may make errors in their forecasts, due to unforeseeable events, but they never make *systematic* forecasting errors. According to the new classical macroeconomics, in general agents forecast the behaviour of economic variables quite correctly. Firms, for example, forecast the price at which they must supply their goods in order to sell their entire production, that is the equilibrium price (which makes supply and demand equal); workers forecast the equilibrium wage, that is the wage at which they must agree to work so that firms can absorb the economy's entire labour force.

In the models of the new classical macroeconomics, therefore, price and wage flexibility is always assumed, which leads the system to full employment. According to this theory, economic policies (monetary and fiscal) are in general useless. In fact, if someone forecasts a depression, that is a decrease in the demand for goods and services, firms lower prices, thereby stimulating demand, and workers accept a lower wage so that firms do not need to lay off any employees. Therefore, there is no need for an expansionary monetary policy.

If firms know that the central bank raises the supply of money in depression, thereby preventing the demand for goods to fall, they do not reduce prices, and workers do not accept a lower money wage; therefore full employment is achieved in any event. If instead agents forecast the depression but not the intervention of the central bank, and such intervention occurs, there is an excess demand for goods and therefore inflation. In the first case an expansionary monetary policy is useless; in the second one it is detrimental.

The only useful economic policy that authorities can implement, according to the new classical macroeconomics, consists in making information available to all agents as quickly as possible. This represents the only way to reduce uncertainty and forecasting errors, and therefore to shorten the process whereby the economy adjusts to sudden and unforeseen shocks.

The conclusion according to which economic policies are useless applies to policies that agents are able to forecast, that is to systematic policies implemented regularly by public authorities. In the real world information and forecasting models of the economy are generally available and they are equally well known by the authorities and by agents (firms, trade unions, etc.). A forecast of a depression or of inflation are known to all these agents. If agents, for instance, know that whenever a depression is forecast the authorities adopt an expansionary monetary policy, such a policy will be useless for the reasons we have discussed. The great majority of the policies formulated by the authorities are systematic, and Keynesian economists suggest precisely these kinds of policies: in a depression, they maintain that expansionary monetary and fiscal policies are necessary, while in periods of inflation restrictive monetary and fiscal policies must be implemented. These policies, for the new classical macroeconomics, are useless.

Non-systematic economic policies, instead, since they are unforeseen, are effective but are also harmful.

Some further thinking about these themes has led many economists to conclude that the hypotheses of the new classical macroeconomics are very far from reality. This has been shown by the fact that these models are unable to explain the persistent and massive unemployment that arose in Europe during the Eighties. The theorists of the new classical macroeconomics and their main exponent, Robert Lucas, reply that this unemployment was largely voluntary and was due to the fact that individuals do not accept to work at the equilibrium wage and, even more important, they do not accept certain types of work.

The new classical macroeconomics, therefore, maintains that: fluctuations in production and employment are caused only by unforeseen perturbations of demand; systematic economic policies are easily forecastable by agents and are therefore useless; unemployment is only due to the free choices of workers who are not willing to work at wage levels that they consider too low.

It has been correctly noticed that such conclusions not only derive from the assumption of agents' 'rational' expectations, but also from the hypothesis that prices and wages are perfectly flexible, which is far from being true. It is sufficient to consider that nominal wages are fixed through collective bargaining agreements over long periods of time (several years) and that firms, especially in the manufacturing sector, change the prices of the goods they sell very slowly. The presence of large inventories and unfulfilled orders shows that firms do not change prices rapidly to reach equilibrium between demand and supply.

In practice, if we abandon the hypothesis of price and wage flexibility, but keep that of rational expectations, the main Keynesian results (that is the persistence of unemployment and the effectiveness of monetary and fiscal policies to achieve full employment and price stability) may hold.

While some authors have stressed this point, others have emphasised that economic agents rarely behave according to the hypotheses of the theory of rational expectations. In fact only big corporations, financial market operators and trade unions can collect a great amount of information and use forecast models, while small firms, single workers and consumers certainly have no possibility of foreseeing the future through such means; moreover, econometric models often produce conflicting forecasts, and therefore agents' behaviour is different according to the models they use. The conclusion is that macroeconomic stabilization policies are useful to achieve full employment and price stability.

Other economists (Malinvaud, Barro and Grossman, etc.), critically revising Keynesian thought with particular reference to the problem of unemployment, show that an excess supply of labour and an excess demand for goods can coexist even with rigid prices and wages. In fact, even when there is an excess demand for goods, firms might find it unprofitable to expand production and hire more workers; therefore excess demand could coexist with unemployment. In this case, the one of classical unemployment, it is necessary to use economic policies which are different from traditional Keynesian ones. A policy which stimulates aggregate demand would not reduce unemployment; this, in turn, would be reduced by policies aimed at raising the profitability of firms, thus stimulating them to increase investment and production.

The comparison between neoclassical and Keynesian analysis leads some authors to attribute the major difference between the two approaches to the fact that the first maintains that prices and wages are flexible, while the second assumes that prices and wages are rigid. For neoclassical economists the disequilibrium between demand and supply gives rise to price changes, while for Keynes it generates changes in production and employment. In general, the difference is attributed to the fact that neoclassical economists assume that the economy is in full employment while Keynes considers a situation of unemployment.

However, as Hicks has shown, the two approaches (the one based on the hypothesis that prices are fixed, and the one assuming that prices are flexible) can be used to analyse both a situation of full employment and one of underemployment. In general, a disequilibrium between supply and demand leads to price changes when markets are close to perfect competition (like agricultural markets or the markets for raw materials). On the contrary, a disequilibrium between supply and demand does not give rise to price changes, but rather to variations in production, inventory accumulation, unfulfilled orders etc. in imperfectly competitive or oligopolistic markets. An oligopolistic firm that sees the demand for its goods fall and thinks the phenomenon is temporary, will simply accumulate inventories; on the other hand, if it experiences an increase in demand, it will make its customers wait for the delivery of the goods. It is therefore necessary to consider the structure of the market in order to analyse the reaction of firms to the disequilibrium between demand and supply.

The debate on the new classical macroeconomics reproposes a theme that we have already analysed, i.e. whether the economy is fundamentally stable and therefore intervention of public authorities is unecessary, or whether it is intrinsically unstable. Keynes insisted not only on the rigidity of prices and wages, but also on the fact that agents take their decisions under uncertainty. The present, for Keynes, represents the link between a known past and an uncertain future.

Authors like Davidson and Minsky have recently insisted on the intrinsic instability of a capitalist economy. According to these authors, modern economies are characterised by the increasingly important role of monetary and financial institutions which create a network of debt-credit relations which increases the instability of the system. Banks are indebted with depositors and are creditors of the firms to which they granted loans; firms are indebted to banks and savers (who purchased their shares and bonds). For instance, if a firm has started to build a plant using bank finance and then faces a sudden rise in costs (for labour and raw materials), it will be unable to make sufficient profits to pay back its loans to banks and may go bankrupt. Banks, not having recovered their loans, may be unable to return the deposited money to depositors. A general crisis could occur which would generate panic, which, in turn, would deepen the initial crisis. These theories echo many economists' fears in the Thirties (Robertson, Hawtrey and others) who insisted on the intrinsic instability of the banking system and on the need of state intervention aimed at regulating economic, and in particular banks', activity.

The above-mentioned authors, together with others who are close to Keynes' approach, believe that a monetary economy works quite differently from a barter economy: the more financial institutions (banks, stock markets and other financial intermediaries) are developed, the more the system is unstable. This is a completely different vision from that of economists, like Friedman and Lucas, who believe the economy has a self-regulating nature.

NOTES

1. We shall come back in more detail to these problems in chapter eleven.
2. Actually, while a reduction of the quantity of money, pursued by means of the various instruments already considered, leads banks to decrease the loans granted to firms and to increase their cost (so that the firms themselves will reduce their investments), an expansion of money supply will augment the banks' supply of loans and will reduce the interest rates. But if firms' expectations on the level of demand and profits are pessimistic, they do not expand investments.
3. As we shall see later on, however, this is a controversial issue.

6 Inflation

6.1 THE CAUSES OF INFLATION

As we have seen, since the Second World War many countries adopted expansionary monetary and fiscal policies in order to keep the economy close to full employment. This, however, led to the stimulation of global demand on global supply, which caused prices to rise. Thus, for the last thirty years inflation has been one of the main problems of industrial economies, leading economists to re-examine the causes of inflation, its effects and the instruments to fight it or, at least, to keep it in check.

As it is well known, by *inflation* we intend a general increase in the prices of goods. Inflation can be *creeping* if the increase is low (usually under ten per cent on an annual basis), or *galloping* if the increase is high (for example thirty per cent a year).

For monetarists inflation is essentially determined by an *excessive increase in the quantity of money with respect to the growth of the production of goods*. An increase in the quantity of money sooner or later gives rise to a demand for goods and determines an increase in prices if the supply of goods cannot be expanded since the economy is close to full employment. The examples that are most often quoted in support of this theory are, as we have seen in chapter three, the importation of large quantities of precious metals from the Americas soon after their discovery and the events that occurred in Germany after both the First and the Second World War.

Instead, for Keynes, we argued that the relevant magnitude is not the quantity of money but global demand, since money might not be spent. In the presence of unemployed resources an excess of aggregate demand over supply causes production to expand. However, when the system reaches full employment, the excess of demand over supply causes prices to rise. In this case we talk of demand-pull inflation. It is obvious however that an excessive expansion in the quantity of money beyond certain limits induces an increase in demand and therefore a rise of prices.

In the last thirty years several economists have pointed to the effects associated with rising costs as the main cause of inflation. If production costs, especially wages and the price of raw materials, rise very quickly, to recover their profit margins firms raise prices (cost-push inflation).[1]

This is what firms did in several Western countries during the Sixties, when they wanted to defend themselves from wage increases, and during the Seventies, when they had to recover the fall in profits following the increase in the price of oil and other raw materials. The excessive increase in wages represents not only an increase in firms' production costs, but leads also to an expansion in the demand for consumption goods and therefore in global demand. If the economy is near full employment, this causes an increase in prices and therefore it becomes difficult to distinguish between cost inflation and demand inflation.

In a study on the behaviour of the British economy from 1861 to 1957, the English economist A. W. Phillips maintained that the causes of inflation could be found mainly in the labour market. From this study it follows that when there is substantial unemployment in the economy, money wages increase little or even decrease. When instead the economy is close to full employment the growth in wages is very rapid. Wages always increase more rapidly as the system approaches full employment. When wage growth is very high, according to the theory of cost inflation, this causes prices to rise.

According to Phillips and to other economists, a possible explanation of this phenomenon may be the fact that a large number of unemployed workers reduces the bargaining power of trade unions such that wages do not increase much. When the economy is close to full employment, the contrary occurs. Another explanation could be that, when unemployment is low, firms find it difficult to hire workers and therefore offer higher wages. The existence of wage drift, this is when the wages that firms actually pay workers are higher than the ones established in collective bargaining agreements, would prove such a statement.

Several economists developed Phillips theory by making other empirical investigations on different countries. Lipsey, for example, found that the rate of growth of wages depends not only on unemployment but also on the increase in the cost of living and on the rate of growth of productivity and profits. It is plausible, after all, that, when these variables increase, trade unions claim wage increases for workers.

As we have seen, popular opinion among economists maintains that,when wages grow on average at a higher rate than productivity, prices increase. On the basis of this observation, Lipsey and others studied the direct relation between prices (instead of wages) and unemployment.

In the Sixties some practical prescriptions of economic policy were drawn from the theory of Phillips and his followers. If one wants to achieve price stability it is necessary for wages to rise at the same rate as productivity. The rate of unemployment that determines such a wage rise must therefore be found. The rate differs from country to country and from period to period, but it is in general equal to three or four per cent of the labour force and is, according to these authors, a rate which is politically acceptable since it is made up by little more than frictional unemployment. If unemployment were further reduced, wages would rise more rapidly than productivity and consequently prices would increase.

This rate of unemployment is constant, but may be reduced by policies that improve labour mobility. If, for instance, there is a demand for workers with specific professional qualifications that the unemployed do not possess, then it is necessary to give the unemployed adequate professional training. In a similar way, the improvement in information about available jobs may reduce unemployment.

Monetarists always maintain that an expansionary monetary policy generates inflation without reducing unemployment. In fact, a price increase caused by an expansionary monetary policy creates expectations for further inflation, that is, it leads economic agents to believe that prices will continue to increase. *Inflationary expectations* cause both trade unions to ask for larger rises in monetary wages and firms to accept such demands because they believe they will be able to absorb the increase in costs by raising, in turn, the prices of goods. However, when firms realise that the cost of labour in real terms has not fallen and that the demand for goods remains stagnant, they will not hire any workers. Therefore, inflation continues and unemployment does not fall. If the authorities continue raising the money supply, the process just examined goes on, inflation worsens, and unemployment does not fall (see paragraph 4.9 in chapter four). Inflation, therefore, is not an alternative to unemployment, but can instead worsen it to the extent that inflationary expectations are self-feeding.

In the Seventies the phenonemon of high growth rates of prices coexisting with high levels of unemployment has been very common. In other words, inflation coexisted with stagnating investment and demand and therefore production and employment, a phenomenon which has been called *stagflation* (stagnation plus inflation).

According to some economists, the causes of stagflation must be attributed precisely to the fact that, even when the level of unemployment is high, inflation feeds itself through expectations. Individuals, facing an increase in prices, foresee even greater price rises in the future. On this basis, trade unions demand substantial wage increases, which in turn generate (both through higher costs and increased demand) further price rises. In practice, in many Western countries trade unions have a remarkable political and contractual power even when there is high unemployment. Several countries adopt automatic mechanisms indexing wages to prices, so that whenever the prices of consumer goods (measured by a given index) rise, wages and salaries also rise automatically. This, in turn, causes a further increase in prices, so that such a mechanism (called indexation) produces a spiral between prices and wages. (In Britain, indexation is not applied to wages but is applied, for instance, to pensions).

Another point today is that many firms operate in an oligopolistic market rather than under perfect competition, and can therefore influence the prices of the goods they produce and sell. Thus, when unions ask for higher wages, even substantially higher ones, these firms concede them in order to reduce conflicts, and then recover the profit margin by raising prices. Inflation would therefore be determined by the *collusion* between industrial oligopolistic firms and trade unions, that are themselves oligopolists. It is clear that, if this is the cause of inflation, the latter can coexist with high levels of unemployment.

Moreover, when there are intense social conflicts,firms experience a fall in profits. Their expectations are pessismistic and therefore they refrain from investing, so that employment grows very little, while firms raise prices in order to recover profits.

Some economists have eventually noticed that policies (both monetary and fiscal) aimed at restricting global demand can generate or at least deepen stagnation given that they can actually cause a contraction in investment, production, and employment, but they are generally unable to reduce the increase in prices significantly.

Another phenomenon which has been widely considered during the last twenty years is inflation imported from abroad. West European countries are poorly endowed of raw materials; therefore they import them from the rest of the world and transform them into final products which are partly reexported. An increase in the international prices of raw materials causes cost inflation; this occurred after 1973, when oil producing countries strongly raised oil prices.

Moreover, as we have seen, a surplus in the balance of payments (due to an excess of exports over imports or to an inflow of capital into the country) determines a rise in the money supply, and may thus generate inflation. The great quantities of dollars outside the United States (the so called *Eurodollars*, or *petrodollars*, relating to the part owned by oil producing countries), originating from the deficit of the American balance of payments accumulated during the last thirty years, often caused inflation in European countries, given that they are easily moved from one nation to another in search of the highest return.

Finally, a devaluation of the exchange rate makes imports more expensive and may, therefore, generate inflation. If sterling depreciates with respect to the dollar, it takes a larger amount of sterling to purchase one dollar. Since the prices of foreign goods are fixed in dollars terms (or in other foreign currencies), more sterling is necessary to purchase a given quantity of foreign goods. In particular, as the international prices of raw materials are quoted in dollars, British firms (that transform raw materials) have to pay more sterling when it depreciates with respect to the dollar, and recover these higher costs by raising the prices of their final products.

Monetarists invariably repeat that in the long run the only cause of inflation is an excessive increase in the quantity of money. Even in the case of cost-push inflation, excessive wage increases are possible only because monetary policy is too expansionary, otherwise firms do not have enough liquidity (that is, money) to grant these increases and would go bankrupt. Unemployment, therefore, occurs and salaries tend to fall. If this did not happen, unemployment would rise even further. Even the possibility for oligopolistic firms to pass the wage rises they have granted on to consumers in the form of higher prices is linked to the fact that they do not experience a considerable contraction in sales when they increase prices, otherwise their profits would fall. Oligopolistic firms do not undergo such a contraction if consumers have a greater quantity of money at their disposal, which makes them able to purchase the goods at the new prices. Wages, moreover, represent the price of labour and therefore, as any other price, rise when the supply of money grows too rapidly.

According to monetarists, the same applies to international inflation, i.e. inflation conveyed from one country to another. In the past, the rise in the prices of raw materials (for example, oil) caused inflation because the United States, in order to allow itself and other industrial countries to purchase raw materials at the new prices, raised the supply of dollars, which is the currency through which international trade is settled.

Even if these considerations are not so neatly specified in the writings of the monetarists, they are implicit in their continuous statement that in the long run prices can increase only if there is an excessive expansion in money supply.

Finally, we may consider a situation that has occurred with some frequence in the past decades: firms facing an increase in their costs of production (for example an increase in wages which occurs only in one country) and producing goods that are exposed to international competition, cannot raise their prices because they would be unable to sell these goods. Let us suppose that international monetary relations are characterised by fixed exchange rates, as in the Fifties and Sixties. A firm that, having experienced an increase in costs, can neither raise prices nor benefit from a devaluation of the exchange rate (see chapter eleven), experiences a fall in its profit margins, and thus reduces investment and lays off workers. The effect of this process is not a rise in inflation, but, rather, an increase in unemployment.

Only a drop in wages which allows firms to fix competitive prices in international markets brings the economy back to full employment. However, a firm that has lost some markets may be unable to regain them immediately, and therefore adjustment occurs only in the long run.

6.2 THE EFFECTS OF INFLATION

In the last century economic literature had already singled out the main effects of inflation; from this point of view recent studies do not contain any new relevant contributions.

Inflation leads individuals not to hold wealth in money or bonds[2] but pushes them to buy real estate, precious metals and stones and goods, whose prices are rising. Likewise, firms are led to anticipate the purchase of their stocks of goods, raw materials, machinery and plant. In order to make individuals hold wealth in the form of money and compensate savers for the devaluation,banks should offer very high interest rates on deposits. In a similar way, the state or the corporations issuing bonds should offer very high interest rates in order to stimulate individuals to purchase them. Therefore, a rise in the quantity of money, generating inflation, raises prices together with interest rates. The Keynesian proposition that an increase in money supply reduces the interest rate holds only when the prices of goods do not change; and actually this is Keynes' hypothesis.

Among other things, a strong inflation puts firms into trouble, because it does not allow them to make correct economic calculations. In fact, when firms set the price of their products, they need to know the prices of the raw materials they buy for the successive production cycle. If they are unable to forecast the price rises of raw materials and of machinery exactly, they are in trouble. Firms generally forecast an increase in costs greater than the one that actually occurs. In this case, they then transfer the expected rises on the actual prices of finished goods, thus making inflation worse. This is the phenomenon of a self-feeding inflation through expectations, mentioned previously.

In an open economy with fixed exchange rates, a price rise reduces the international competitiveness of goods. If the prices of British goods increase (and the exchange rate of sterling with respect to the foreign currencies remains unchanged), British products become more expensive for foreigners, who thus choose to purchase goods from other countries.

Hence British exports fall. It is evident that, for a country to keep its international competitiveness, absolute price stability is not important. Rather, it is sufficient that its prices rise no faster than those of the other countries competing with it in international markets.

An exchange rate devaluation raises the competitiveness of exports. For instance, a devaluation of sterling with respect to the German mark implies that a larger quantity of sterling is purchased with one mark, so that, even if the prices (in sterling) of British goods do not change, the Germans can purchase British goods with a smaller quantity of marks. Therefore a country whose prices grow too fast can devalue the exchange rate in order to reestablish its foreign competitiveness. However, as we have noted, such a devaluation makes imports more expensive and thus worsens domestic inflation. Therefore there is the danger, confirmed by past experience, that a vicious circle of *inflation-devaluation-inflation* is created. A country that is unable to keep its price rises in line with those of its competitors devalues its currency, but in such a case, even though it restores its export competitiveness, it worsens the domestic price rise and must devalue the exchange rate once again; thus it becomes still more difficult to break the vicious circle.

Finally, as it is well known, to a considerable extent inflation redistributes income among social groups. A price rise puts firms, tradesmen, professional men, real estate and precious metals owners in advantage while it damages social groups with fixed incomes, since their purchasing power falls. As we have already mentioned, after the Second World War various countries introduced automatic mechanisms of wage indexation linking wages to price rises. Nevertheless, if indexation is granted to all workers, this leads to a spiral of price and wage increases which becomes difficult to control. On the contrary, if the mechanism of automatic adjustment is granted only to some categories of workers, a privileged group is created, which is not damaged by inflation, while the incomes of other workers fall in terms of their purchasing power because of the rise in prices.

In some periods indexation has been extended also to other types of income, like interests on bank deposits or bonds. Indexed bonds are characterised by the fact that a bond's yield is linked to the inflation rate, in the sense that it rises when the inflation rate increases and diminishes when the inflation rate falls.

The experience of some Latin American countries, where indexation mechanisms are extended to almost all the sectors of the economy, shows how inflation self-feeds itself at a rate unknown to Europe: the prices of goods triple or quadruple well within a year.

6.3 ANTI-INFLATIONARY POLICIES

The policies suggested by economists to fight inflation are different according to the causes that generate the phenomenon. If inflation derives from an excessive increase in the quantity of money, then it is necessary to reduce the expansion of its supply. As we have pointed out, monetarists suggest letting the money supply grow at a constant rate, in order to give agents a stable economic framework.

Keynes focused mainly on the problems of depression, but Keynesian economists, applying his type of analysis to inflation, suggest that the way to combat it is by restricting aggregate demand, not only through monetary but also fiscal measures, namely through public spending reductions and tax increases.

As we have mentioned, past experience shows that monetary policy, while scarcely effective in an expansive direction, is much more effective in a restrictive direction: for this reason it is said to have *asymmetrical effects*. For instance, an increase in the interest rate on advances (of the central bank to commercial banks) or of the official discount rate reduces the resort of banks to central bank financing. Banks therefore have less liquidity and consequently raise the interest rate on loans to firms and cut down their credits to them. Firms curtail investment, which reduces aggregate demand. The same consequences are produced by an increase in the legal reserve ratio, which reduces the capacity of the banking system to multiply deposits and hence curtails the total volume of banking deposits. Thus banks, having less liquidity, cut down loans to firms and raise their cost. Also in this case firms reduce investment.

Measures addressed to curtail public expenditure have an immediate effect in reducing aggregate demand, as the Keynesian multiplier works either in an expansionary or in a contractionary way. Finally, as far as taxes are concerned, an increase in direct taxes causes a reduction in individuals disposable income and hence in consumption. Alternatively, an increase in indirect taxes (on consumption or on traded goods) can lead to a rise in prices, because, when goods are taxed with duties, sellers try to raise prices in order to transfer the real burden of taxes on consumers. A rise in indirect taxes can thus result in higher inflation.

When inflation is caused by an increase in costs, in particular wages, it is necessary to keep the dynamics of such variables under control. As we have mentioned, according to Phillips and his followers, this is possible only by keeping a certain unemployment rate in the economy (three or four per cent); therefore, through an appropriate mix of monetary and fiscal policies, aggregate demand must be preserved at a level corresponding to such an unemployment rate. Further increase in demand would result in inflation; reductions would imply an excessive and socially unacceptable level of unemployment.

Notwithstanding the combined use of fiscal and monetary policies to achieve simultaneously full employment and price stability, stagflation, that is the coexistence of a high rate of inflation (and a consequent balance of payments deficit) with high unemployment, appeared with growing frequency in the economies of several Western countries in the Sixties and Seventies. This led various economists to believe that fiscal and monetary policies were unable to reach the targets of internal and external equilibrium simultaneously. From the Seventies on, given the return to a floating exchange rate system, the possibility of changing the exchange rate (devaluation or revaluation) adds to the short run instruments available to governments. However, even this instrument has proved to be inadequate to fight stagflation.[3]

Since the Sixties several economists stressed the necessity of an *incomes policy*. This, however, was intended in many different ways. Some economists conceived it as a means to keep the dynamics of wages in check (essentially, thanks to trade unions endorsing a policy of self-control of wage increase requests following government suggestions), so that, on average, wages would not rise faster than productivity.[4] Other economists, instead, gave a broader meaning to the term 'incomes policy', thinking that it should represent a self-discipline for all social groups, avoiding a situation where agents' money incomes exceeded, on the basis of current prices, the production of goods, hence resulting in inflation. In such a sense incomes policy implied not only self-discipline for trade unions with regard to wage claims, but also for firms and tradesmen, who should not raise the prices of their products in an attempt to raise their incomes (i.e. profits).

Some authors have also suggested introducing a mechanism which would be agreed upon by social groups to keep the dynamics of incomes in check and to supervise the application of the agreement.

These short considerations allow us to consider the connection between incomes policy and another instrument to fight inflation: *price policy*. This consists in authorities keeping the price dynamics in check, in order to avoid excessive price rises. Such a policy is not new; historical experience has shown that it can lead to the hoarding of goods and to the creation of black markets. However, this policy can also be intended as a form of self-control, or self-discipline, and thus leads to the same results of incomes policy. In fact, containing the rise in the price of goods necessarily implies a control of increases in incomes, since the prices of goods include costs, among these labour costs, and the profits of producers, intermediaries and final sellers.

In Western economies a form of self-discipline has been often lacking and the pressure of various social groups to obtain a greater share of national product has caused inflation. In that case the analysis of the inflationary process coincides with that of the underlying *social dynamics*, namely of the behaviour of agents and particularly of organised social groups, that play such an important role in modern economies.

NOTES

1. Let us think of national income as a pie which is divided between wages and profits (keeping other incomes aside). If the pie doubles and both wages and profits double, the distribution of the pie remains unchanged in the sense that the share of wages in national income and that of profits do not change. In this case, we usually state (but the statement is not exempt from objections) that firms do not increase the prices of the goods they produce. If, instead, the share of wages increases at the expense of profits, firms raise prices.

   The condition that total wages must increase in proportion to national income in order for prices not to increase is usually expressed by affirming that the wage rate (that is, the average salary of a single worker, given by total wages divided by the number of workers) must increase at the same rate of the average productivity of labour (that is, national income divided by the number of workers). More briefly: salaries must increase in line with productivity.

2. Fixed-yield bonds have the same outcome of cash. Shares yield a variable income. Inflation, therefore, could raise the profits of the companies which have issued shares, and the companies could decide to distribute a higher dividend to shareholders.

3. On this issue, see chapter eleven.
4. It often happens that in the sectors where productivity rises more rapidly, for instance in manufacturing, wages grow at the same rate of productivity. But, due to an imitation effect, wages in the sectors where productivity growth is low (agriculture and services) grow at the same rate of wages in manufacturing. This leads to a price rise of products in the sectors where productivity is more sluggish, e.g. in agriculture and services. Thus a *sectoral inflation* arises. However, the growth of those prices usually brings about further wage claims in all sectors, raising inflationary impulses and transforming sectoral inflation into generalised inflation.

7 Cycles, growth and development

7.1 ECONOMIC THEORY IN THE THIRTIES

Keynes' *General Theory* focused on short run problems and the possible existence of an underemployment equilibrium. Long run phenomena and in particular economic growth were neglected. The observation of reality, however, showed that basically two problems remained to be analysed: national income grows and hence it is necessary to identify which factors lead to its expansion; growth does not occur in a regular way, as national income increases in some periods and falls in others. Moreover, growth sometimes takes place at a faster rate and sometimes at a slower one. The first problem relates to growth and the second one to business cycles. It is necessary to single out the factors that determine each phenomenon.

Classical economists, and particularly Ricardo and Marx, had considered the problems of the business cycle and of growth. These themes were abandoned by the Neoclassics, who concentrated on exchange. Even when dealing with production, the Neoclassics analysed a static context, neglecting the problem with regard to the growth of production over time.

In the first decades of this century the Austrian economist Schumpeter called the attention of economists to cycles and growth by formulating a theory that attributed income growth essentially to two factors: *technical progress* and *entrepreneurial functions*.

Technical progress consists of the invention of a new good or a new method of production. Schumpeter asserted, on the grounds of what had happened during the Nineteenth century and in the early Twentieth century, that, when an invention occurs (e.g. a particular type of engine, electricity or the aeroplane is invented), a strong increase in investment takes place (because firms produce the new goods in large quantities) and therefore a great increase in income and employment occurs as well. Nevertheless, the essential elements for such investment to occur are the ability of entrepreneurs and their willingness to undertake risks.

Since the most relevant inventions take place at irregular time intervals, also investment (and consequently the rise in production and employment) occurs at irregular intervals. Hence income and employment expand through cyclical fluctuations.

Schumpeter showed how technical progress consists of the creation of new goods and of the birth of new industries, that he termed 'creative destruction'. This implies the destruction of jobs in the old industries and the creation of jobs in the new ones. For instance, the production of wagons and horses is abandoned, while that of locomotives and railway carriages develops. It is obvious that problems of professional and geographical labour mobility (i.e. the transfer of workers from the aging industries to the new ones) arise, which can generate unemployment, at least in the short run.

Lederer has developed Schumpeter's ideas, underlining the distinction between static firms and innovative firms. The waves of technical progress reduce the growth of production and employment in the static firms and at the same time curtail employment in the innovative firms (that substitute capital with labour), thus creating unemployment in the economy as whole.

The banking system plays a crucial role in Schumpeter's growth theory. In fact, growth requires not only innovative entrepreneurs willing to take risks, but also bankers' willingness to finance the massive investment that the innovative entrepreneur must make in order to introduce mass production of the new goods into the economy. By himself, the innovative entrepreneur does not have (from savings and self-financing) the huge financial means necessary to produce a new good or to introduce a new method of production on a large scale. Therefore bankers face some risk when they decide to finance an innovative firm.

7.2 MULTIPLIER-ACCELERATOR BUSINESS CYCLE MODELS

Beginning in the Thirties in the wake of Keynesian analysis, some economists started considering business cycles. They formulated a theory ascribing the alternation of expansion and depression to the joint operation of two mechanisms: the income *multiplier* and the *accelerator*. As we already know, the first one is the mechanism by which an increase in investment causes an expansion of global demand (for goods and services) and hence of national income. On the other hand, the accelerator is the phenomenon through which a rise in aggregate demand generates investment. For example, if a firm producing bicycles in a certain year records an increase in demand of fifty bicycles compared to the previous year and considers this rise to be permanent, it will make the investment necessary to produce fifty more bicycles a year permanently. The accelerator, then, is the phenomenon through which firms facing an increase in demand invest in order to expand their productive capacity, buying new plant and machinery that permits them to adjust the supply to the new level of demand.

Starting from a situation where unemployed workers are present, an increase in investment, through the multiplier, produces an expansion of the demand for goods and of national income. In turn, the increase in demand, through the accelerator, leads firms to carry out investment in new plant and machinery, in order to expand productive capacity.

Hence the following succession of events takes place: initial investment produces an increase in national income (i.e. in aggregate demand); the increase causes new investment, that in turn generates income, and so on. Therefore a phase of expansion occurs during which national income, employment and all the main macroeconomic variables (consumption, investment, etc.) grow, until full employment is achieved.

At this point an increase in investment always generates a higher demand (through the multiplier), but firms cannot expand production any more. On the other hand, full employment can determine an increase in wages, since firms have difficulty in finding workers on the labour market and attracting them by offering higher wages. The wage rise reduces the firms profits, and can worsen their expectations and make them cut down investment. However, a fall of investment produces, through the multiplier, a reduction of employment and of aggregate demand.[1] Such a fall will, in turn, through the accelerator, make firms reduce investment,[2] and so on. A phase of depression thus follows expansion.

Usually the beginning of a new phase of expansion does not occur automatically, since, as Keynes had pointed out, the economy can stagnate in an underemployment equilibrium. Therefore, measures to expand aggregate demand (public investment, reductions in taxation) are necessary so that investment recovers and a new phase of expansion starts again.

This analysis explains how the interaction between the multiplier and the accelerator determines cyclical fluctuations. Growth, *vice versa*, is attributed to the increase in population and to technical progress; the latter enables the production of a greater quantity of goods with the same number of workers. These two factors imply that every phase of expansion ends in a level of national income that is higher than the one in the previous phase: i.e. every peak is higher than the preceding one. For example, when the economy attained full employment in 1980, the level of production (of national income) was higher than that of the closest year in which the system had reached full employment (let us assume it was 1977), because of the increase in population and of technical progress achieved from 1977 to 1980.

Hence, income fluctuations do not occur along a horizontal straight line – which would imply a stationary trend – but rather along an increasing trend. Alternatively, it can be said that growth (i.e. the increase in national income) takes place through cyclical fluctuations.

This type of analysis has been formulated in the period going from the Thirties to the Fifties by several economists such as Samuelson, Hicks, Frisch, Tinbergen, Fanno, Goodwin, Kalecki, Phillips and others.

7.3 HARROD'S THEORY OF GROWTH; HANSEN'S HYPOTHESIS OF LONG TERM STAGNATION

At the end of the Thirties the English economist Harrod developed an analysis similar to the one we have just considered. Harrod, besides analysing business cycles with the instruments of the multiplier and the accelerator, transfers Keynesian analysis to the long run. Let us suppose that the economy grows in a way that aggregate demand and aggregate supply expand at the same rate. In this case the economy expands along an equilibrium path, that could coincide with a succession of Keynesian underemployment equilibria. In fact, aggregate demand and supply are always equal, since they grow at the same speed,[3] but equality between the two, as Keynes underlined, does not necessarily imply full employment of the labour force.

On the basis of Keynes' conclusion that there is no endogenous mechanism leading equilibrium national income (or actual income) to be equal to potential income, Harrod maintains that there is no way by which the equilibrium growth of national income (i.e. the growth by which aggregate demand and supply grow *pari passu*) will automatically coincide with the growth of income that ensures full employment. For instance, it could occur that, given the rate of growth of population and that of technical progress, a five per cent yearly growth rate of national income would be necessary to guarantee continuous full employment (i.e., starting from a situation of full employment, the continuous absorption of the new active population). However, it can occur that the rate of growth of equilibrium income, that allows aggregate demand to grow at the same pace of aggregate supply, is of three per cent. In this case the equilibrium expansion of the economy would imply growing unemployment.

Some aspects of Harrod's theory had been anticipated by the Swedish economist Cassel, while the American economist Domar came to conclusions similar to those of Harrod some years later, by an independent route.

On the ground of Harrod's analysis, Hansen and other authors, called *stagnationists*, argued that the tendency of the economy to stagnate in a situation of underemployment is not only a short run phenomenon, but also a long run one, as the economies of industrial countries tend to grow while under-utilizing the resources at their disposal, that is keeping workers unemployed and machinery unused. Hence there is a tendency toward a *secular stagnation*.

Furthermore Hansen pointed out that the principal factors that produced a very rapid growth in the Ninenteenth century were being exhausted by the Twentieth century. Above all he mentioned the cultivation of new fertile lands in the United States due to the colonisation of the West, which was completed by the end of the Nineteenth century, the growth of the population and technical progress, that he thought would slow down in the Twentieth century. However the forecasts of the stagnationists have been largely disproved by following events.

Harrod and Hansen, however, underlined the necessity of continuous intervention on behalf of the state, that, through adequate fiscal and monetary policies, can attempt to keep aggregate demand at the level corresponding to full employment. These considerations confirm and strengthen the need for Keynesian policies such as those that were advocated during the Sixties at an operational level by the economic advisers of the President of the United States of America.

7.4 THE NEOCLASSICAL THEORY OF GROWTH

Harrod's analysis conformed to the Keynesian spirit predicting the tendency of the economy to stagnate in underemployment. Beginning from the mid-Fifties the American economist Solow, among the others, returning to some ideas already expressed by the Dutch scholar Tinbergen, elaborated a neoclassical model of growth based on the flexibility of wages and consequently excluded the possibility of underemployment equilibrium growth. In fact, Solow asserts that, if the economy grows along such a path, this equilibrium cannot last for a long time. The existence of unemployed people on the labour market causes a decline in wages. Consequently, firms absorb unemployed workers by either investing or adopting techniques that use relatively more labour and less capital. The reduction in wages continues until unemployment is completely absorbed; then the economy goes on and grows along a full employment path.

In such a way the contrast between Keynes and the Neoclassics concerning short run problems is reposed in the theory of growth. In fact, in the Keynesian spirit, Harrod's reply to Solow was that his mechanism for achieving full employment assumes a downward flexibility of wages which, as a matter of fact, does not exist, given the existence and the power of trade unions. However, even if such flexibility existed, a decline in wages, far from leading the economy to full employment, would cause a reduction of demand for consumption goods and hence of aggregate demand, determining a fall in production and a consequent increase in unemployment.

According to the Neoclassics it is doubtful whether the Keynesian difficulties relating to an insufficient level of aggregate demand remain also in the long run.[4] They believe that in any case the long run rate of growth of national income is essentially determined by factors influencing supply, i.e. the production of goods. Therefore it is not correct to examine the problems of growth through the mechanisms of the multiplier and the accelerator, which are typical tools of short run analysis, where demand plays a central role. Since the production of goods depends on the quantity of inputs (capital and labour) used in production and on technical progress, the growth of national income depends on the growth of capital (plant and machinery), on the increase in the labour force (i.e. the number of workers) and on the rate of technical progress. The growth of capital is determined by the economy's investment, the increase in labour force depends on the growth of population, and technical progress depends on the flow of investment and innovation.

Through empirical studies Solow and other authors tried to determine which portion of the increase of national income in the United States (or in other countries) in a certain period was due to an increase in population, to an increase in capital (i.e. to investment) and to technical progress.

However, for different reasons, in the Sixties these studies aroused growing scepticism. One of the main objections is that technical progress is usually embodied in new capital goods. Given that inventions (e.g. a train or a car) are introduced into the economy through investment, as Schumpeter pointed out, technical progress cannot be disjoined from capital accumulation, nor can one separate the effects that the two phenomena have on the increase of national income.

Several authors have pointed out that investment is the vehicle through which inventions penetrate the economy, and some investment (for instance in scientific research) stimulates invention. Thus, the result that it is impossible to separate the effects of technical progress on the growth of national income from those of capital accumulation is reinforced.

Several economists have developed empirical studies directed at measuring the growth of different countries, and together at specifying its causes in relation to the above criteria. The task, however, presents numerous difficulties of a statistical nature.

7.5 THE REVIVAL OF THE CLASSICAL THEORY OF GROWTH

In the Sixties, while the neoclassical approach was being applied to the theory of economic growth, some economists (e.g. Joan Robinson) referred to the classical tradition and in particular to Marx as a framework for the problems of business cycles and growth. In this respect, some authors underlined that the cyclical course of the economy is strictly linked to the conflict between firms and workers concerning income distribution.

In a situation of underemployment wages are low, given the abundance of labour supply (on behalf of workers) compared to labour demand (on behalf of firms), and hence profits are high. The classical economists assume that profits are almost completely saved and reinvested, since capitalists use only a small part of their income for consumption, and that wages are at a subsistence level and as such are almost totally consumed. Hence, high profits make firms invest. This determines an increase in production and employment. Therefore a phase of expansion follows, lasting until the economy reaches full employment.

At this point firms demand for labour turns out to be greater than supply, and the difficulty of finding workers pushes firms to raise wages. The increase in wages generates a fall in profits, that in turn reduces investment and consequently national income and employment. Hence a phase of depression follows.

According to this analysis, the capitalist economy expands only by recreating periodically a certain number of unemployed workers, which Marx called the 'industrial reserve army'. By restraining the increase in wages, the industrial reserve army allows profits and investment to rise, thus regaining impetus. However, Mrs. Robinson suggested nothing assures that expansion lasts until full employment is achieved, since entrepreneurs' expectations could become pessimistic and the rate of investment could drop. Such a consideration introduces Keynesian elements in a Marxian-type analysis.

According to this framework, in the long run the rate of growth is determined by the increase in population and by technical progress, which, as we have mentioned, each time allow the ceiling of full employment to be reached at a higher level of income than the previous one. The Keynesian consideration, recalled by Mrs. Robinson, that pessimistic expectations can prevail, reducing investment, and therefore leading to underemployment growth applies also in the long run. Namely, growth could leave workers unemployed and machinery idle, as Hansen and the stagnationists feared.

In this vein the position of the British economist Kaldor is partly different. According to Kaldor, once the economy has reached full employment after an expansion, a phase of depression may not necessarily follow; on the contrary, a stage of regular growth in national income could occur, without cyclical fluctuations, along a path assuring the full employment of resources. In the multiplier-accelerator model previously examined, when the economy reaches full employment, investment always generates demand (for goods and services) through the multiplier, but, since production (i.e. supply) cannot be expanded, the excess demand leads to an increase in prices. This, in turn, reduces demand to the level of supply. At this point, especially if monetary and fiscal policies succeed in regulating the evolution of aggregate demand keeping it in line with the evolution of supply (i.e. production) determined by the increase in the population and the rate of technical progress, an equilibrium growth can start (where aggregate demand and supply grow *pari passu*), assuring at the same time the maintainance of full employment.

7.6 LEWIS' MODEL

Even the model of the British economist Lewis has a Marxian derivation. The model considers the process of industrialisation of a country where a large part of the population is employed in agriculture. Lewis assumes that the latter consists of a poor, non mechanised agriculture; the population, therefore, is willing to move from the countryside to towns. Jobs are available in industry, since industrial wages are low, but they are always higher than the earnings individuals obtain by working in agriculture.

If an industrialisation process starts, Lewis points out that workers leave the countryside and move into towns. As long as a population exists that is willing to move from agriculture to industry, the supply of labour is abundant, and wages in industry do not rise or in any case grow very slowly. Furthermore, since the population employed in agriculture is overabundant, the fact that part of it moves to town does not determine a fall in agricultural production.

In this situation, where population moves from the primary activity to industry and wages do not grow, industrial profits are high and firms reinvest them continuously. Such a process entails high profits, high investment and hence high rates of growth of industrial production and of national income. The process leads to a continuous expansion of the industrial sector and lasts until people are unwilling to move from agriculture to industry. As we have argued, the population exodus from the countryside does not reduce agricultural production. *Per capita* income in agriculture (namely the earnings of an agricultural worker) increases as the population moves into industry. The incentive to transfer ceases only when a small part of the population remains in the countryside, and therefore the revenue that an individual can get by working in agriculture is approximately equal to the wage that he would receive in industry.

When the labour force reserve is exhausted, the demand for labour of industrial firms exceeds the supply of labour. Thus wages rise, profits decline and a consequent reduction in the rate of growth of national income occurs. From then on the feasible rate of growth of the economy is given by the increase of the population and the rate of technical progress.

This type of development had been analysed by Marx with reference to the industrialisation process of Britain in the Seventeenth and Eighteenth century. As Marx pointed out, the transfer of the population from the countryside to towns was only spontaneous to a small extent, as labour conditions in the factories were extremely tough and wages very low. The British Government enacted laws that in practice forced countrymen to move to town in order to work in the factories.

Lewis' model has been adopted to explain the development of some European countries after the Second World War. For instance in the early Fifties the Italian population still employed in agriculture was about fifty per cent of total population, while nowadays it represents not more than ten per cent. A similar process took place in Japan. On the contrary, the reserve of agricultural labour appears to be completely exhausted in Britain and in the United States, where for many years the population employed in agriculture represents a percentage below four per cent of total population.

Historical experience, moreover, shows that the process described by Lewis may stop before the labour force reserves in the countryside are exhausted. Industrial wages are higher than the earnings workers get in agriculture, and this is the reason why people leave the countryside and move to town. Industrial workers, getting higher wages, consume a greater amount of foodstuffs than agricultural ones. Therefore the migration of the population from agriculture to industry gives rise to an expansion in the overall demand for foodstuffs.

However the supply of foodstuffs cannot meet the higher demand, given the difficulty of raising agricultural production in the short run, and therefore the price of foodstuffs increases. This phenomenon occurred in several Latin American countries, that passed through a first phase of industrialisation, and has been called *structural inflation*. The price rise can determine wage claims together with political and social tensions, with a consequent slowing down of investment and of the rate of growth of production.

Sometimes the process outlined above gives rise to higher imports of foodstuffs. Hence, if a country is unable to counterbalance greater imports with an adequate expansion of exports, a balance of payments deficit occurs instead of inflation. In turn, the deficit contributes to slacken development, because authorities, in order to limit the deficit (since they do not have infinite currency reserves to finance it), must reduce growth, perhaps with restrictive monetary and fiscal policies.

To avoid this phenomenon, it is necessary to mechanise and modernise agriculture, which raises the production of foodstuffs. These, however, are processes that are difficult to accomplish in the short run.

Another cause that may interrupt the growth process described by Lewis is represented by the fact that workers may form trade unions, which could make industrial wages increase consistently even before the labour reserve in agriculture is exhausted. The increase in wages, reducing profits, makes investment fall and curbs the economy's rate of growth.

7.7 ECONOMIC DEVELOPMENT AND INTERNATIONAL TRADE

Lewis' model is a supply model where the engine of growth is given by the availability of workers which keeps wages low. This, in turn, leads to large profits, high investment and a high rate of growth in national income. An implicit assumption in Lewis' model is that aggregate demand is always at a level high enough to completely absorb the supply of goods by using all the existing plant and industrial labour. In other words, the model does not consider the typically Keynesian problems of an insufficient aggregate demand due to a low propensity to consume or a low level of investment (determined, for example, by the pessimistic expectations of entrepreneurs), because it is believed that these problems are typical of industrial economies.

As a matter of fact, an abundant labour supply is a necessary condition to start industrialisation, but it is not a sufficient condition, because it is also necessary that aggregate demand grows continuously in order to sustain the expansion in production.

Different authors, on the grounds of past experience, underline the positive role that foreign demand (i.e. exports) can have for development. The theory of international trade maintains that complete freedom of trade allows different countries to exploit the benefits derived from specialisation in production.[5] This occurs by reducing costs, favouring the growth of production and of national income.

The increase in exports leads firms to utilize more productive capacity if unemployed resources are present in the economy. Moreover, a continuous increase in exports pushes firms to invest in new plant and machinery, i.e. to expand existing productive capacity. If the supply of labour is abundant, as Lewis assumes, foreign demand stimulates development through the following events: high exports cause high investment, which, given an abundant supply of labour, determines a rapid rate of growth in national income. Furthermore, high investment also favours development by stimulating technical progress (see the previous considerations in paragraph 7.4).

Nevertheless, for the reasons we have already mentioned, the rapid growth of the economy can cause an increase in the imports of foodstuffs, and, since industrial activity consists in transforming raw materials – which industrialising countries do not always have – into finished goods, this may also raise the imports of raw materials. This generates a balance of payments deficit, unless the developing country is able to export finished products in an amount sufficient to pay for higher imports. For this to happen, the country must be able to sell its products at competitive prices on international markets. Namely, in a fixed exchange rates regime, it is necessary that the prices of its goods grow more slowly than those of the goods of the other countries competing with it on international markets. If productivity grows more or less at the same rate in all countries, it is necessary that in the developing country wages grow more slowly than those of the competing countries;[6] this condition often occurs in a country which is in its first phase of industrialisation.

If the developing country cannot keep its exports competitive, their volume declines and they are not sufficient to compensate for greater imports. In order to reduce the balance of payments deficit the developing country is obliged to adopt restrictive fiscal and monetary policies that reduce the rate of growth of national income.

7.8 THE PROBLEMS OF DEVELOPED ECONOMIES

While countries in an early phase of industrialisation have a large share of the population employed in agriculture, highly industrialised countries (e.g. Britain, the United States, Germany) have only a small percentage of total population working in agriculture (even less than five per cent) and hence do not have a great number of workers available for the expansion of industry. The supply of labour is fuelled only by the natural growth of the population (given by the difference between births and deaths), which, in developed countries, is rather low. Since these countries invest abundantly, the shortage of workers represents an obstacle for the growth of national income.

Some countries (e.g. Germany, Switzerland, Belgium) have tried to overcome labour shortage by allowing foreign workers to immigrate; others (like the United States), albeit favouring immigration in the past, now restrict it strongly. The reason for this is given by the political fear that immigration could create social tension and conflicts with the local population. Trade unions, on the other hand, fear that an increase in labour supply would cause the wages of national workers to fall. However, experience has shown that this fear is largely without foundation, because immigrated workers normally fulfil functions that are different (usually more humble) than those of national workers, thus creating two distinct categories of workers (immigrated and national ones) that do not compete with one another.

Developed countries with strong immigration may continue to grow according to Lewis' model. On the contrary, in those countries where immigration is limited and the natural growth of the population is low, the rate of growth of the economy is determined by the other factors, namely capital accumulation and technical progress, and is inevitably lower.

Some authors have pointed out that in an advanced economy in the course of development the percentage of population employed in industry remains stationary or diminishes, while that employed in the service sector rises. This phenomenon has been named "tertiarization" of the economy.

The growing importance of the service sector from the point of view of employment is due to the fact that the number of workers in industry falls, because technical progress, essentially taking the form of mechanisation, automation and computerization, allows to expand production with only very small increases in employment. On the other hand, this occurs to a much lesser extent in the service sector. It is true that also in the service sector there are examples that go in the opposite direction (the substitution of small shops by supermarkets, of restaurants by self-services, the introduction of computers in banks and in public offices), but in many branches of the service sector mechanisation cannot be applied. The most common examples are schools and hospitals, where the number of teachers per student tends to grow as much as possible, as well as that of doctors and nurses per patient.

Hence in highly industrialised societies (e.g. the United States) young workers at their first job are largely absorbed by the service sector rather than by industry. In industrialising economies (e.g. Italy in the Fifties) the population which is expelled from agriculture does not move to industry (as Lewis' model postulates), but, rather, it is directly absorbed by the service sector (and by the building sector, that in some countries is a branch of industry with a high intensity of labour), since the growth of industry essentially occurs through the increase in productivity.

As we have already argued, one of the main consequences of this is the following: wages in industry usually grow at the same rate of productivity while wages in the service sector tend to increase at the same speed of industrial ones due to an imitation effect. However, as productivity in the service sector grows slowly for the reasons we have already mentioned, firms producing services (for example barbers, restaurants, hotels, hospitals, private schools, transport) are forced to raise prices. This creates a type of inflation, called *sectoral inflation*, through which the prices of services rise while those of industrial goods remain stationary.

The strong increase in the price of some services reduces their demand, but, given their importance to society, the state ends up by producing them directly (e.g. education and health) and supplying them at a price below costs or free of charge. Given the difficulties of raising the tax to GNP ratio beyond certain limits, this determines increasing deficits in the budgets of the state and in those of local government. As we have noticed, in the long run these deficits may generate inflation.

7.9 STATE INTERVENTION FOR GROWTH

In the last decades state intervention in industrial countries in favour of growth has increased and so has its economic impact. As we have already noticed, the first type of intervention consists of the use of stabilisation policies (fiscal and monetary) to attain full employment of the available resources (men and plant). In addition to this intervention of a short run nature, there are structural ones, that are directed at stimulating capital accumulation and technical progress (for example direct investment in the field of scientific and technological research) and to regulate labour supply, controlling immigration, as we have already mentioned.

Other structural interventions are those concerning education and industrial policy.

In the majority of industrial countries the government organises education, which is compulsory and free of charge until a certain age. Particular attention is given to professional training, which consists not only of the education granted to young people before they get a job, but also of the help given to employed workers to keep up to date. Education is considered one of the fundamental factors of development, since it represents the formation of the so called 'human capital'.

Another sphere of intervention is regional and urban planning. Industrialisation, by determining a massive transfer of people from countryside to town, generates a strong expansion of cities, which has some negative aspects. Therefore public authorities intervene to assure that urban expansion occurs according to a certain plan (the town plan) preserving green areas in every quarter; that an efficient system of public transport (undergrounds, etc.) is created, so that the transfer time from home to work is reduced; and speculators are prevented from buying building land just to sell it later on at high prices; that cheap housing is built for the poor.

Recently, the idea that industrial activity should not be left only to the initiative of private firms, but must be partly oriented by the state, has been put forward. Since industrialisation tends to concentrate in some areas, while others remain depressed, the state may grant incentives (loans at low interest rates, tax reductions, sunk funds) to firms investing in depressed areas. In this case, economists say that the state implements a *regional policy* or a *policy of regional development*. The state may pursue similar targets by locating investment in particular zones directly through public firms. In the last decades the latter have become more and more diffuse in Europe. Other forms of intervention may be directed at sustaining declining industries (e.g. coal mining in Britain, which is declining because the demand for coal is falling, since it has been substituted by oil and electricity). In this case the state favours the transfer of workers from the declining sectors to the expanding ones. This requires training or reeducating workers, in order to promote their mobility. In this case economists talk of an 'active labour policy'.

In some countries the coordination of all forms of intervention directed at promoting the growth of the economy has been called 'economic planning'.

7.10 ECONOMIC GROWTH AND EMPLOYMENT

In the last twenty years unemployment has been very intense in European countries, leading some economists to talk of mass unemployment. In the period going from the beginning of the Seventies until now, unemployment has been low in the United States and Japan (from three to six per cent of the labour force), while on the other hand European unemployment has always been above ten per cent, and has grown constantly.

Economists have widely discussed the causes of unemployment, especially why it persists in presence of sufficiently high rates of growth of GNP. In general, we used to think that in a depression both the rate of growth of GNP and the growth of employment fall (or at least stagnate), whilst the opposite occurs during an expansion. On the contrary, the experience of the Eighties has shown that income and employment do not necessarily move in the same direction, and it is possibe to have 'growth without employment'.

Some authors attribute European unemployment in the Seventies and Eighties to the rapid increase of technical progress. Although some years ago several analysts were inclined towards this thesis, today the general attitude is more prudent.

New technologies,e.g. computers, save both manual and intellectual labour and hence destroy employment, but, on the other hand, they create jobs in the new industries that produce computers and related goods. Even if on the whole some unemployment may arise, it can be absorbed by the service sector that is in continuous expansion and which presents many activities that have a high intensity of labour (schools, hospitals, assistance to elderly people, gymnastics and sports, tourist activities, etc.). The process of creative destruction, that, according to Schumpeter, is generated by technical progress, can result in unemployment in the short run, but this can be reabsorbed quite rapidly.

The question is whether a stable relation exists between the growth of productivity (defined as the ratio of GNP to the number of employed workers) and that of employment or alternatively between the growth of productivity and that of production. In the Sixties one of the most accredited theories was that of Verdoorn-Kaldor-Arrow (Dutch the first, British of Hungarian origin the second, American the third); according to these the average productivity of labour rises faster the more rapidly production grows. In fact, a rapid increase in production determines growth in the average size of firms, that can introduce new and more advanced machinery. This implies an increase in firms' productivity leading to scale economies. Moreover, workers using new machinery acquire the skill only rather slowly and the more they use it the more their productivity grows. The more rapidly production grows, the quicker the productivity of workers rises as a consequence of *learning by doing*. Such a phenomenon is particularly important in manufacturing, but, since the other sectors (agriculture and services) are complementary to manufacturing, the relationship may spread to the whole economy.

However experience has shown that there is no simple relationship between the growth of production and the evolution of employment. In the Fifties and Sixties almost all industrial countries introduced massive automation. Negative effects on employment were feared, but they failed to occur. In fact, during this period, nearly all industrial countries achieved strong increments in both productivity of labour and employment, and hence a rapid growth of GNP was coupled with the expansion of employment, particularly in the service sector. On the contrary, in the last twenty years European countries have recorded low increases of GNP and higher ones in labour productivity with a consequent fall (or very scarce rises) in employment. Historically we have: phases of increases in both productivity and employment (such as Italy in the Fifties); phases of increase in productivity and stagnation or reduction of employment (for instance Britain in the Seventies); phases of stagnation of productivity and growth of employment (such as the United States in the Seventies). Hence the law of Verdoorn-Kaldor-Arrow is disproven.

Another version, of a neoclassical nature, attributes the different evolution of employment in the United States and in Europe in the last twenty years to the different flexibility that the markets of labour and capital have in the two regions. The flexibility of the labour market is given not only by wage flexibility but also by the mobility of workers across different firms, sectors and geographical areas, by professional mobility, the possibility of reducing working time and of introducing part-time jobs, etc. . Actually, it has been pointed out that a large part of the youth unemployment in Europe is of an intellectual type, and it is voluntary. The same applies to a great extent to female unemployment. Therefore, these two types of unemployment coexist with the immigration of Third World workers. In the United States in the last fifteen years more than eighty per cent of jobs have been created in the service sector and especially in traditional areas like hotels, restaurants, hospitals, private police, where wages are relatively low also because part-time jobs are diffuse. Moreover, even in Japan during the Eighties part-time or definite-time jobs have generally been created, in contrast with the country's tradition of providing a life-time job.

This interpretation raises some points. During the last century and until the First World War empirical investigations show a strong link between wages and employment: wages declined during recession and increased during expansion. In various countries after the First World War wages started being indexed to the cost of living, even if fluctuations in income and employment continued to have a great influence on the level of wages. After the Second World War, until the Sixties, the data seem to confirm Phillips' theory or its variants. A rise in unemployment is correlated not with a fall in nominal wages but with a fall in their rate of growth. Besides, from the beginning of the Sixties the evolution of wages appears to be linked not only to the rise in the cost of living but also to the increase in productivity. The sectors recording a more rapid growth of productivity often allow their wages to rise to the same extent. Through an imitation process, the same wage increases spread to low productivity sectors. Even if in several countries these mechanisms have faded in recent periods, in the last twenty or twentyfive years a relationship between the growth of wages and the employment level is often lacking. As a matter of fact wages are sticky and firms facing short run fluctuations in demand have not reduced wages but rather dismissed some workers or reduced working hours.

Phillips theory has been abandoned in favour of the 'implicit contracts theory', which gives a more sophisticated explanation of wage rigidity and of the fluctuations in employment, by analysing the behaviour of firms and workers at the microeconomic level.

If this is the case, it is difficult to argue that the causes of unemployment in Europe are the dynamics of wages and a lack of flexibility in the labour market.

Alternatively, the Keynesian interpretation attributes the different dynamics of employment in Europe and in the United States to the evolution of aggregate demand in the two regions. In the last fifteen years the United States has constantly pursued an expansionary fiscal policy: it has increased the federal budget deficit financing it either by raising the money supply (in the Seventies) or foreign indebtness (in the Eighties). European countries, on the other hand, due to the already huge budget deficits and to the foreign constraint (which for them is much more cogent), have pursued restrictive, or at least non expansionary, fiscal policies, while some, like Germany, have accumulated enormous balance of payments surpluses. However, Japan has not pursued expansionary policies, has accumulated remarkable foreign surpluses, and yet has a very low level of unemployment.

No investigation of a statistical or econometric type can allow us to choose definitely between these different models, given the complexity of the elements and variables involved.

The Keynesian interpretation gives rise to an objection, that we have already examined, stating that in a fixed price regime an excess supply of labour and the excess demand for goods can coexist in a multiplier model. While in the presence of an excess demand for goods, firms can find it inconvenient to expand production and employ more workers; hence the excess aggregate demand can coexist with unemployment. In this case, namely if it is possible for unemployment of a classical type to exist, it is necessary to adopt economic policies different from the traditional Keynesian ones. In fact a policy stimulating global demand does not reduce unemployment; rather, it would be more appropriate to adopt measures directed at increasing profitability, in order to induce firms to expand investment and production.

Naturally the exponents of the new classical macroeconomics assert that it is not necessary to adopt any form of economic policy, given that European unemployment is of a voluntary type, because unemployed workers refuse to work at what would be the equilibrium wage and, above all, they refuse to accept particular types of job.

More wisely it can be thought that, in the presence of high levels of unemployment, governments should take into account policies regulating demand and also those which regulate supply, especially labour supply and productivity.

In fact, the rate at which new technology is introduced into the economy depends largely on the governments political decisions, besides those of large corporations, given the growth in the public sector and the programmes of industrial reorganisation, reconversion, professional retraining, which depend largely on public funds. Moreover, due to the weight that public administration has inside the service sector, the growth of employment in this sector is considerably influenced by political decisions.

Naturally the introduction of new technology does not always result in unemployment. If the computerisation of production processes allows us to save labour thus generating unemployment, it will also raise employment in the industries that make computers. For instance, the diffusion of personal computers has this result. In this respect, the role of the state is very important: one may consider the effects of a programme of the large introduction of computers into the public sector (including personal computers in schools) on global demand and employment.

The process of the introduction of inventions into the economy is controlled more and more by goverments and large corporations, which are able to regulate and manage technical progress, thus controlling the level of employment. In many countries such a policy is also influenced by the behaviour of organised social groups and in particular by trade unions.

Therefore the demand management policies determine the rate of growth in GNP, while policies regulating productivity essentially determine the level of employment.

In recent years, economists have paid particular attention to the reduction of working time and to the introduction of part-time jobs, as a method of reducing labour supply, which has already been experimented within various countries. Some authors have pointed out that measures of this type, and especially the introduction of part-time jobs, while reducing the supply of labour, also tends to generate a new supply of labour of those who were previously unwilling to find a job. The net result of this phenomenon could be either a fall or an increase in the aggregate supply of labour. Moreover, measures of this type could have a negative impact on the demand for labour, to the extent that they make firms' costs of production rise.

Both the diffusion of part-time jobs and the reduction in working time can contribute to reducing unemployment, if they are carefully implemented. The reduction of working time, for instance, must be introduced in line with the economy's growth in productivity. Obviously, this may either lead to wage increases or to a reduction in working hours.

Moreover, the reduction in working time that has progressively occurred over the last century has been an antidote to unemployment, in that on the one hand it has balanced the effects of productivity rises and on the other hand it has stimulated the demand for both consumption and investment goods.

The more serious objection that can be raised to the reduction of working time is that a country exposed to international competition cannot adopt such a measure without taking into account what the other countries do.

NOTES

1. In fact, using the multiplier mechanism, as an increase of investment allows employment to expand and generates an increase in global demand (for goods and services), a reduction of investment determines a conctraction of employment and of aggregate demand.
2. According to these theories, a firm facing a fall in the demand for its goods curtails production leaving plant and machinery idle, but, if it considers such a fall as permanent, it will tend to reduce its productive capacity. This does not occur through the destruction or the sale of the machinery owned by the firm, but, rather, through a reduction of the sums set aside for the depreciation allowance of machinery. Therefore, the latter will not be replaced when it is obsolete and should be discarded.
3. If at a given moment aggregate demand and supply are equal and then grow at a same rate, they continue to be equal.
4. The problems of interest rate flexibility, of money neutrality and of the effectiveness of monetary policy for achieving full employment are also reproposed for a growing economy.
5. See chapter eleven.
6. If productivity grows more rapidly in a developing country than in competing nations (e.g. because the latter have an older industrial structure), also wages could rise in the developing country more rapidly than in the others, without reducing its competitiveness.

8 The problems of underdevelopment

8.1 THE PROBLEMS OF UNDERDEVELOPED ECONOMIES AND THE VICIOUS CIRCLE OF POVERTY

In recent decades attention throughout the world has been drawn to the problem of the enormous differences in living conditions of industrial countries and underdeveloped or developing ones. Since the beginning of the industrial revolution, while the countries of North America and Western Europe and only a few others had enormous increases in per capita income as well as in the general welfare of the entire population, the vast majority of the remaining countries have living conditions that are at the border of, or barely exceed, the level of dire poverty.

The majority of countries in Asia, Africa and Latin America are considered underdeveloped. Although these countries are notably different from each other as far as economic, social and political structures are concerned, they all have certain characteristics in common. Their principal activity is agriculture, which employs a very high share of the population (sometimes more than fifty per cent). Generally speaking, agriculture is poor and unmechanised and displays a strong overabundance of labour, or *disguised unemployment*.

Other characteristics of underdeveloped economies are the low level of education and of technical training of the labour force, the scarcity of infrastructure (roads, harbours, railways, telecommunications, etc.), the

108

inadequate development of industrial activity. All these factors contribute to making per capita income – i.e. income that individuals have at their disposal – very low. Income is almost entirely consumed and thus saving is extremely low. Consequently, investment is small, also as a consequence of the scarcity of infrastructures and of the general lack of entrepreneurship.

Keynesian analysis cannot be applied to these countries. Unemployment is structural, in antithesis to that of industrial countries (Keynesian unemployment). For Keynes, unemployment is necessarily accompanied by the presence of unutilized industrial plant and machinery; in this situation an expansionary fiscal and monetary policy determines an increase in global demand and consequently in production, leading the economy to full employment; that is, it allows to utilize fully industrial plant and machinery and employs all the existing labour force. In a Keynesian framework, unemployment is caused by insufficient global demand.

On the other hand in underdeveloped countries, unemployed workers are present even when industrial facilities and machinery are fully utilized. This is due to the fact that there is not sufficient plant and machinery to employ all the labour force. Therefore, once the full utilization of facilities has been reached, measures for expanding global demand would generate price increases in spite of the high level of unemployment, because production cannot be raised. The problem of underdeveloped countries therefore is not one of expanding global demand, but rather of creating industrial facilities and machinery, that is industrial ventures, which can help to absorb structural unemployment.

In underdeveloped countries unemployment usually occurs in the form of hidden (or disguised) unemployment in the agricultural sector, where the amount of work that could be done by one worker is distributed among four or five workers. Part of the population employed in agriculture could leave the sector and move to town without reducing agricultural production, as Lewis' model maintains.

Due to these characteristics, developing countries risk remaining caught in a vicious circle that the Swedish economist Myrdal called the *vicious circle of poverty*. Low incomes cause low saving, which, together with the lack of infrastructure and the population's lack of industrial entrepreneurship and skills, is responsible for the low level of investment. Consequently, growth in production and income remain very modest.

Moreover, the scarce capital and the few technicians existing in underdeveloped countries often end up by emigrating to industrial countries where there are more favourable working conditions. It is not easy to change these conditions and to develop enterprises in countries where traditions, mentality and social structure are not those of an industrial society but rather of a feudal one (as in certain Asian countries) or of a tribal one (as in some countries of Africa).

Models like Lewis' or such as those based on the leading role of demand (both foreign and national) explain the process of industrialisation of certain countries which are at an intermediate stage of development (as for example Italy in the Fifties or Spain and Greece since the Eighties), but they do not apply to the majority of underdeveloped countries where the process of industrialisation never got off the ground, for the reasons we have mentioned.

8.2 DEVELOPMENT POLICIES

There are two types of intervention which are deemed to be necessary for making industrialisation take off in an underdeveloped country; these may be foreign or national. Foreign intervention consists of financial help (low interest loans or donations) from industrial countries to developing ones, in order to allow the latter buy equipment and machinery abroad and pay foreign technicians for implementing their development programmes. National intervention, instead, should concentrate on agriculture, infrastructure and industrialisation.

In developing countries vast areas of land are often owned by absentee landlords; or they are broken up into an excessive number of separate allotments. In both cases, cultivation methods are extremely outdated. The modernisation of agriculture is one of the primary targets of a developing country. In fact, as we have seen examining Lewis' model, it is only by raising food production during development that inflation can be avoided. Modernisation of the agriculture requires both considerable investment for reclaiming land, for irrigation and mechanisation, for creating farms (including cooperatives) run according to managerial methods. Reforms of the farm structure are difficult to implement because they clash with the interests of large landowners and with the

110

individualistic mentality of small farmers (who for instance could refuse to join in cooperatives).

In the last twenty years large corporations, often multinationals, have modernised agricultural structures on a large scale in several developing countries. Thus, the creation of irrigation systems, the reclamation of land, the large scale introduction of agricultural machinery and of chemical fertilisers and even of genetic engineering methods have determined an enormous increase in worldwide agricultural production, to such an extent that the phenomenon has been called a 'green revolution'. If on one hand this has solved the food problem for many countries (even if problems relating to the transportation and distribution of food products often remain open), on the other it has also created new imbalances. The more advanced management of firms has considerably reduced the need for workers in agriculture. A large number of people have abandoned rural areas and moved to towns, many of which have undergone an extensive and rapid expansion which has created serious problems of congestion, housing shortage, inadequate transportation, difficulty of employment, etc. .

Another type of intervention which should be carried out in developing nations consists of the creation of large scale programmes of public works, aimed at creating infrastructure (the improvement of soil conditions, the exploitation of water sources, the creation of roads, railways, harbours, etc.). These types of intervention are usually easier to be implemented because they clash much less with preexisting interests and consolidated structures.

Intervention which is directly aimed at industrialisation must try to attract foreign investment and develop local investment. Regarding the former, it has often been the case that large multinational firms have carried out investment in underdeveloped countries which was aimed only at exploiting natural resources, such as plantations, mines, etc. . This investment does not favour the development of backward countries, because it does not stimulate a process of industrialisation. Instead, investment ought to create industries aimed at transforming these countries' raw materials.

One very delicate problem raised by economists regards the choice of the sectors in which to invest and the choice of the production techniques to be employed, i.e. whether it should be labour intensive or capital intensive techniques.

111

Opinions on these matters vary greatly; recently there has been a tendency to advise underdeveloped countries to adopt technologies with a high or at least an intermediate labour intensity. This tendency is based on the empirical observation that in the last few decades employment in underdeveloped countries has risen very little even when there was a considerable increase in national product. That is, the increase in production came about mainly through increases in productivity due to the introduction of advanced technology. Several economists have criticised the dangers arising from this situation which is called 'development without employment'.

It is not easy to develop local entrepreneurship in countries where the mentality and the set of values are different from those of an industrial society. It is necessary to supply local firms with financial help (low interest loans, tax relief, etc.) as well as with real incentives (technical assistance, professional training, etc.). It is also important to develop the population's education, paying special attention to technical and professional training. Expenditure in education, representing the so called investment in human capital, is one of the most important factors for starting a process of development.

8.3 BALANCED AND UNBALANCED GROWTH

One of the most famous debates on the theory of development of less advanced countries concerns the problem of whether development should be balanced or unbalanced. According to the theory of balanced growth, due to Nurkse, industrial investment should not be concentrated only in one sector, but rather should be directed simultaneously to different sectors.

If a firm producing for instance mens' shirts is created in an underdeveloped country, the newly employed workers of the shirt firm will have much higher incomes compared to when they were unemployed or underemployed in agriculture. Therefore, they will be able to buy not only shirts, but also food, clothes in general and so on. However, as in the country there are not enough firms to produce these goods, demand determines either an increase of prices or, if the goods are imported, a deficit in the balance of payments. For the reasons we have already mentioned, in this case an increase of demand cannot lead to an expansionary process of income and production of a Keynesian nature.

On the contrary, if investment determines the simultaneous creation of other firms producing goods that workers can purchase with their income, both inflation and balance of payments deficits do not occur. In fact, if for instance a shoe industry, a clothes industry and a food plant are created simultaneously, the problems we mentioned do not arise, because every worker of each industry can purchase the goods that are produced by the other industries.

The American economist Hirschman and others have criticised Nurkse's theory of balanced growth, maintaining that the creation of an 'integrated development area' like the one mentioned in the previous example leads in practice to a self-sufficient area that consumes what it produces. If the workers of a factory consume all (or almost all) the goods they produce, this leads to the creation of a self-sufficient area which does not stimulate growth outside itself. If, instead, factories are created outside an organic project related to an integrated area as in the first example we mentioned, in which there is only one firm producing men's shirts, the demand for other goods on behalf of the workers of that firm will stimulate the creation of other factories producing other goods. This continuous stimulus is the only factor that can keep growth going on.

On the basis of past experience it is difficult to tell which of the two types of growth appears to be the most viable. There is no question that some types of investment, like the exploitation of mines or of large plantations, do not trigger any development process. Other types of investment, instead, can produce the impact mentioned by Hirschman. For instance, the creation of a plant producing lorries can stimulate the creation of small firms producing lorry pieces or fittings: fans, tyres, and so on. According to this example, the creation of a firm generates also a demand for investment goods, together with one for consumption goods on behalf of the firm's workers.

8.4 INTERNATIONAL TRADE AND DEVELOPING COUNTRIES

While, as we have seen, international trade can favour the industrialisation of a country at an intermediate stage of development, it represents an obstacle for more backward countries.

113

Actually the latter need to import investment goods to foster their own industrialisation and, in order to pay for them, they must necessarily increase their exports. Moreover, developing countries essentially export primary products, i.e. farm produce (coffee, cocoa, sugar, cotton, etc.), and raw materials (iron, copper, oil, etc.), both of which face two main difficulties: their prices are extremely unstable and the terms of trade (i.e. the price ratio) between primary products and manufactured goods in the long run tends to fall.

The *instability of prices* stems from the fact that both demand and supply of these products are subject to sharp and sudden variations. If, for example, difficulties in transportation and trade are foreseen, due to political reasons or to a war, a tendency arises to buy raw materials and farm products on behalf of those countries which do not have them. Hence, a sudden increase in the demand for these goods occurs and, consequently, a sharp increase in prices takes place. Variations in the supply of farm products due, for instance, to unpredictable weather conditions are even more frequent. A big harvest of a certain product brings about an expansion of its supply, which of course drives its price down, whereas a poor harvest has the opposite effect.

Sharp variations in the prices of primary products also make the currency proceeds from their sales fluctuate. In turn, these proceeds represent the main resource with which developing countries can buy equipment and machinery from industrial ones.

In order to reduce these difficulties, many developing countries have created specific agencies with the task of regulating the supply of farm produce. Every time the supply of a given product exceeds its demand and, consequently, its price would undergo a sharp decrease, these agencies buy large quantities of the product and store them, avoiding a sharp drop in its price. On the other hand, in case of a poor harvest, when demand exceeds supply tending to drive the price of the product up, these agencies supply the market with the stored goods. When stocks cannot be preserved, either because they consist of perishable foodstuffs or when very good harvests occur for some years in a row, the agencies partly destroy them.

Another serious problem affecting developing countries is the *secular decline of the terms of trade between primary and manufactured (industrial) products*; this is due to the fact that the prices of the latter increase far more rapidly than the prices of primary products. Hence, in

114

exchange for a given quantity of their goods, underdeveloped countries end up by purchasing increasingly smaller quantities of industrial products, i.e. equipment and machinery that are vital for their development.

There are two main reasons for this phenomenon. First, thanks to technological progress, industrial countries have largely replaced primary products with synthetic ones: for example, silk, wool and cotton have been replaced by synthetic fibres; timber and metals by plastic. This leads to a decrease in the demand for primary products and, as a consequence, to a fall in their prices.

The second reason is that whereas primary goods are generally produced in competitive conditions, industrial products are produced by oligopolies. In developed countries the existence of big oligopolistic firms and powerful trade unions constantly drives the prices of products up, since large firms, in order to reduce conflicts, allow for wage increases and then make up for them by raising the prices of the goods they produce. This mechanism does not usually work in developing countries where trade unions are weak and the firms producing primary products (for example, food) operate in a competitive framework and thus cannot influence the price of their products. However, some developing countries have recently tried to reach oligopolistic-type agreements among themselves in order to raise the price of primary products. Oil-producing countries, for example, joined forces and often acted in conjunction through their organisation (OPEC) in fixing oil prices.

Finally, developing countries' exports are harmed by the agricultural protectionism of industrial countries, especially that of the EEC, which subsidises its national agriculture and levies duties on imports of foreign farm products.

For these reasons, developing countries face serious deficits in their balance of payments, which, in turn, lead to considerable indebtedness *vis à vis* industrial countries; the situation becomes even worse when development is started, because it inevitably needs the continuous import of equipment and machinery which in general developing countries cannot repay through higher exports.

That is why industrial countries are generally asked to increase their aid to developing ones and to reduce agricultural protectionism. UNCTAD (the United Nations Conference of Trade and Development) is the organisation created for these purposes; it aims at developing trade between industrial and developing countries on more favourable bases for the latter. In practice, however, over the past years little has been done to liberalise trade between the two groups, mainly because developed countries continue to protect their agriculture both through import duties on farm products and through subsidies to national agriculture.

8.5 CURRENT GROWTH PERSPECTIVES FOR DEVELOPING COUNTRIES

The foreign debt of developing countries *vis à vis* the banks of the industrial ones, and particularly U.S. banks, has now come to a point where developing countries are unable to repay not only their debts, but also the interest due every year. Economists and politicians are studying the possibilities of reversing this trend and helping developing countries to grow.

According to some economists, developing countries should try to expand their exports and, to do so, they should industrialise and produce manufactured goods. This is not an abstract idea: in fact, during the last years, several developing countries started following this approach.

These countries are called NICs (Newly Industrialising Countries) and include several countries belonging to the Pacific Ocean area, like Hong Kong, Taiwan, South Korea, Singapore and some Latin American countries like Brazil and Mexico.

Many firms have been set up in these countries producing and exporting manufactured goods (shoes, garments, etc.).This was made possible by the fact that these countries have lower wages than the industrial ones and a longer working week; thus, they can produce at lower costs and their prices are lower than those of industrial countries.

Of course, NICs generally produce manufactured goods such as shoes, clothes, etc., which require only elementary technologies (i.e. those goods which are in a 'maturity stage', according to the product cycle theory),[1] since NICs are unable to carry out research and development autonomously and receive technological know-how from industrial countries. During the Seventies and the Eighties, multinational companies often found it convenient to locate factories producing textiles in NICs. More recently still, it has been the case of more advanced technology factories producing for instance toys, electric materials, electronic goods, etc..

At the moment, it is unclear whether in the future NICs will be able to produce manufactured goods which require more advanced technology, while other developing countries, which today only export agricultural products and raw materials, will be able to produce manufactured goods and export them.

Optimists argue that this will be possible, but there is also a pessimistic opinion. According to these economists, NICs' experience cannot be repeated in developing countries in general. They argue that industrial countries would be unable to absorb exports coming from the developing ones, should these exports increase all at the same time. NICs are in fact only a few countries, some of them having a rather small population. Let's think of India and China: if they were to develop their exports, could the industrial world absorb them?

Pessimists argue that developing countries, in order to restore balance of payments equilibrium and to reduce indebtedness with industrial countries, must concentrate their efforts not so much on developing exports but rather on reducing imports. In other words, developing countries should produce consumption goods inside their borders, replacing imports. In short, they should undertake *import substitution* rather than *export promotion*.

Developing countries could produce clothes, shoes, electrical household appliances, cars, etc., even through old technologies which exploit more labour and less capital (i.e. through less automatisation and computers compared with industrial countries' firms).

In developing countries, corporations would probably face higher costs than those of industrial countries, and they would be therefore forced to sell goods at higher prices. Developing countries would be unable to export to industrial countries, and consumers in developing countries would always tend to import goods from abroad (i.e. from the industrial area), given that they cost less. Therefore, developing countries should adopt appropriate protectionist policies to avoid these problems and to develop a national industry. Pessimists think that it will take a long time for developing countries to develop and in the meanwhile they will have to pursue both protectionist and autarchic policies.

Other experts put forward *plans to reduce the present indebtedness of developing countries* and to make sure that such indebtedness will not occur again in the future. These plans, named after the politicians or economists who proposed them (for example, the Brady plan, after the U.S. Secretary of Treasury), usually envisage the *rescheduling* of the loans supplied to developing countries by Western banks. Rescheduling consists of reducing the interest rates on these loans; given the impossibility of receiving the interests due within the prescribed term, banks voluntarily give a discount to debtor countries.

Some of these plans envisage an automatic reduction in interest (that the debtor countries must pay to banks) every time that the situation of the world economy is such that the debtor nations, i.e. the developing countries, can hardly export their goods and therefore they do not earn adequate proceeds in dollars.

NOTES

1. See chapter eleven.

9 Welfare economics, the theory of economic policy, econometrics and experimantal economics, the problems of centrally planned economies

9.1 PIGOU'S WELFARE ECONOMICS

Theories dealt with in the preceding paragraphs concern the so called *positive economics*: they aim at explaining how the economy works and analyse the effects of government intervention. For instance, the law of demand states that when the price of a good increases there is a decrease in the quantity demanded. Keynesian theory asserts that an increase in investment, both public and private, gives rise to an increase in income and, consequently, in production and employment.

Economists wonder whether economics could include, besides the positive propositions mentioned above, also *normative propositions*, that is suggestions and rules of behaviour concerning the intervention of public authorities. The problem concerns assertions such as 'it is a good thing to redistribute income from the rich to the poor' or 'it is a good thing for certain industries to be nationalised instead of being left to the private sector' and so on.

While certain economists think that these types of propositions have no scientific character since they imply *value judgments*, that is moral judgments, other authors have instead tried to give normative propositions a scientific basis.

In 1920 the British economist Pigou attempted to identify a single principle that should inspire economic policy measures. He identified such a principle in the maximisation of social welfare.

The concept of *social welfare* derives from the British utilitarian tradition, whose chief representative was Jeremy Bentham. According to this school, each individual's utility, i.e. his pleasure or psychical satisfaction, was *measurable*, and the utilities of different individuals were *comparable* and *summable*. According to these assumptions social welfare was defined as the sum of the utilities of single individuals, *who were assigned the same capacity for satisfaction*.

However, not all welfare can be measured on a monetary basis: for example, the utility enjoyed by an individual when going for a walk or looking at a pleasant view cannot be measured through a market price. That is why Pigou considered only that part of welfare which can be measured on a monetary basis and which he called *economic welfare*. The theory that economic policy measures should be governed by the principle of maximising economic welfare instead of social welfare was justified through the assumption that economic welfare represented the main part of social welfare and consequently an increase or a decrease in the former would produce a variation in the latter in the same direction.

As economic welfare is the sum of the utilities of all individuals, deriving in turn from the consumption of goods, economic welfare depends upon the quantity of goods produced, that is upon national income and, in particular, both upon its *volume* and its *distribution* among individuals.

According to Pigou, an increase (or decrease) in the volume of national income would always determine an increase (or decrease) in social welfare, unless an income redistribution harming the poor took place.

For a given volume of income a change in its distribution would give rise to an increase or to a decrease in social welfare depending upon the direction of the redistribution. If the redistribution took place from the more well-off to the less well-off it would raise welfare; if, on the other hand, the redistribution went from the less well-off to the more well-off, welfare would fall. This conclusion derives directly from the assumptions regarding the comparability of utilities and the equal satisfaction capacity of different individuals. A redistribution of income from the rich to the poor causes an increase in the latter's utility greater than the utility fall experienced by the former, as the needs of the poor are more intense than those of the rich. For example, if a given policy reduces the income of an individual from 105 to 100 pounds a month, while the income of another person passes from 952 to 957 pounds, the first individual must give up satisfying basic needs (for instance eating), and undergoes a marked utility diminution. At the same time, the second individual satisfies luxury needs, i.e. needs that are less important than those of the first individual. He therefore obtains a slight utility increase which is certainly lower than the utility loss of the first individual. Thus overall social welfare declines.

Pigou's criterion allows to compare various economic policy measures on the basis of their effects and to choose those that maximise social welfare. The latter rises each time the volume of national income increases or an income redistribution from the rich to the poor occurs. Starting from this basis it is possible to determine e.g. whether it is worthwhile to increase social expenditure (public housing, free education, etc.) or to nationalise a company.

However, each time an economic policy measure affects simultaneously both the volume and the distribution of national income and does so in opposite directions, Pigou's criterion does not allow us to establish whether a social welfare increase is achieved or not. For example, a tax on higher incomes whose proceeds are used to build cheap housing raises social welfare as it redistributes income from the rich to the poor. However, in case of an excessively high tax, the rich could curtail investment, provoking a drop in production, that is in national income, and thus diminishing social welfare. Apart from these cases, Pigou's principle allows to compare various economic policy measures according to their effects and to identify the one that maximises social welfare.

9.2 THE CONTRIBUTION OF ROBBINS AND PARETO OPTIMALITY

Pigou's theories had a remarkable impact on the scientific environment of his age, especially in the Anglo-Saxon world. But in the same period different approaches, mainly related to the Italian economist Vilfredo Pareto and to the British one Lionel Robbins, were beginning to be known and to gain approval.

Both authors rejected the assumption underlying Pigou's theory, i.e. that different individuals' utilities could be compared and therefore summed. But, while Pareto still defined a criterion for choosing among different economic policy measures, Robbins' criticism went even further, affirming that any criterion aiming at selecting the most appropriate economic policy measure lacked scientific ground.

In his work *An Essay on the Nature and Significance of Economic Science*, published in 1932, Robbins referred to the 'continental thought' (in particular to German and Italian economists) and asserted that suggestions, advice and any other normative proposition could not have the objectiveness of a scientific proposition since they were affected by value judgments. Robbins denied the fact that economics could 'generate within itself a series of principles which are compulsory for practical policy', believing that the ultimate aims of economic policy have nothing to do with science and depend upon *ad hoc* value postulates. Accordingly, the task of economic science should be to identify the most suitable means to attain certain goals and not to choose among different goals, which should be left to politicians and not to economists. For example, politicians are those who have to decide whether a more egalitarian income distribution should be implemented or not; the economists' task is limited to the identification of the most appropriate means to reach either one or the other target.

Despite the fierce criticism of this school of thought, economists went on formulating recommendations and rules of behaviour for economic policy, while at the same time identifying the criteria that should inspire economic policy intervention. As we already mentioned, Pareto, for instance, did not give up trying to define a target for economic policy measures, even though he refused the utilitarian conception underlying Pigou's theory.

Let us assume that the entire community faces a given situation and that, by means of an economic policy measure, it is possible to reach a new situation where no one is worse off but at least someone is better off: according to Pareto, it can be asserted that for the whole community the new situation is preferable to the previous one. As the economic measure does not bring any damage to anyone, no individual records a fall in utility, while someone (at least one person) has an increase in his utility. The assertion that the new situation is better than the previous one does not therefore entail any comparison among the utilities of different individuals.

Economic policy measures should therefore tend to achieve a situation which could not be abandoned without making at least one individual worse off. In the economic literature this position has been called *Pareto optimum.*

Even though he refused Pigou's assumptions on utility, Pareto succeeded in establishing a criterion for the selection of economic policy measures. Nonetheless, the fact that he abandoned the assumption that the utilities of different individuals could be compared made his criterion much *weaker* than Pigou's: in practice, most economic policy measures entail advantages for certain individuals and disadvantages for others. In this case Pareto's theory does not allow us to establish whether the new situation is better or worse than the previous one for the community; in order to do so, Pareto thought that the utility decreases and increases of different individuals should be compared and this could be done only referring to moral or political principles, that is to non-scientific criteria.

For example, if an economic policy intervention slightly reduces the income of an extremely rich individual while simultaneously increasing that of many poor ones, Pareto asserts that this does not entail an increase in social welfare. It represents an increase in social welfare from an ethical point of view, but not from a scientific one. In fact, it is not possible to compare scientifically the utility reduction of the very rich individual with the utility increase enjoyed by the poor.

In order to express Pareto's criterion in terms that are more easily comparable to Pigou's, we can note how the former deems that any economic policy intervention raising the volume of national income without affecting its distribution amongst individuals brings the entire community to a better situation. In fact, if a measure makes some individuals (at least one) better off without making anyone worse off, this means that in the new situation some individuals (at least one) have at their disposal more goods than they had before the measure was undertaken, and that no one has fewer goods than he had before. The volume of national income has therefore risen, while its distribution has remained unchanged.

Instead, a measure making some people (even one person) worse off modifies the distribution of national income among individuals. According to Pareto, it is not possible to compare situations characterised by a different distribution of income, as this would require a comparison of the utilities of different individuals.

The 'weakness' of Pareto's criterion therefore becomes apparent: according to his position, the 'optimum' is a situation in which the volume of production is at its maximum. On the basis of such a principle, however, a situation can be defined as an optimum only with reference to a comparable situation (i.e. one characterised by a lower volume of national income but by the same distribution) and not to any possible situation (that is, also to those characterised by a different income distribution). As it was correctly remarked, Pareto's criterion identifies a situation of *relative optimum* and not an absolute optimum, because there is not a unique optimum, but an infinite number of such situations, each relating to a different distribution of national income among individuals in a community.

9.3 THE COMPENSATION PRINCIPLE

The so called *compensation principle*, developed by Barone, Kaldor, Hicks and other economists, tried to overcome the limits of Pareto's criterion. These economists consider a measure benefiting some individuals while harming others: if the individuals who are better off compensate those who are worse off and, after paying the compensation, have still some benefit left, it can be asserted that for the community the new situation is better than the previous one.

Under this point of view, the compensation principle represents a true extension of Pareto's criterion. In fact, once the compensation has been paid, some individuals are better off and nobody is worse off; hence, for the community the new situation is preferable to the previous one without having to compare the utilities of different individuals.

However, the compensation principle can also be interpreted in another way: according to some economists, in order to define a situation as being better than the previous one, it suffices for the individuals who are better off *to be able to compensate* those who are worse off. Whether the compensation must actually be paid is a question that should be settled according to political principles. The only task entrusted to

124

economists is that of ascertaining that those who are better off are able to make the payment.

Such an approach however does not solve all the problems: in case the compensation is not paid, some of the individuals are better off and others are worse off. Hence, in order to assert that the new situation is preferable to the previous one for the entire community, a criterion is needed allowing to compare the utilities of different individuals. The main problem of welfare economics is therefore reproposed and still remains to be solved.

9.4 THE SOCIAL WELFARE FUNCTION AND INTERTEMPORAL OPTIMISATION

The so called *social welfare function*, introduced by the American economist A. Bergson and subsequently developed by Allais, Samuelson, Arrow and others, represents an attempt to solve the problem we have just considered in a different way from the ones analysed so far.

These authors assume that every individual has his own preference scale concerning the many possible alternatives regarding the economic organisation of society. Moreover, they attempt to construct a scale of preferences for the community on the basis of individuals' preference scales. The scale of preferences for the community is named 'social welfare function' and also represents a criterion for choosing among economic policy measures, as it permits to rank them according to their effects.

Besides, Bergson notes that the scale of preferences of each individual reflects personal preferences on production and the distribution of income among various social groups. That is, each individual has a scale of preferences for the many possible distribution scenarios (more or less egalitarian).

While some economists, like Bergson and Samuelson, construct a social welfare function by adding the functions (or scales) of preferences of single individuals, others, like Arrow, build it through the method of *voting* (in other words, individuals are invited to vote to express their preferences among different alternatives relating to the economic organisation of society). In the first case the social welfare function reflects the preferences of all individuals, while in the second one it only reflects the preferences of the majority. In both cases, however, when shifting from individual to collective preferences, the difficulties arising are such that the construction of a collective scale of preferences is virtually impossible. Moreover, the problem of comparing the utilities of different individuals is once again felt, because when passing from individual preferences to collective ones it must be decided which weight should be given to each individual's preferences. If we give the same weight to each of them we express a value judgement which is more or less similar to the one implicit in Pigou's assumptions, that is that all individuals have the same capacity for satisfaction.

One branch of studies regarding welfare economics which originates from the analysis of the British mathematician and economist F. Ramsey (1928) and his American colleague Irving Fisher attempts to single out a criterion for choosing among the vast number of different types of economic policy measures which benefit or damage not only members of the existing population, but also those who are not yet born. In this case, it is necessary to establish a criterion of *intertemporal optimality*.

Within this field we find the theory of optimum saving (or investment), which was developed by several authors (Samuelson and Solow, Koopmans, Cass, von Weizsäcker, etc.) in the wake of Ramsey's and Fisher's analysis. This theory attempts to determine, on the basis of a rational criterion, in which part the available resources should be assigned to consumption and to investment. By consuming less today, it is possible to invest more and thus increase the level of consumption for future generations, and vice versa. The Pareto criterion appears to be inadequate for selecting among measures of this kind, and the same can be said for the social welfare function. In order to create a scale of preferences, it would be necessary to know the preferences of individuals who are not yet born, which is obviously impossible. Economists dealing with this problem have assumed that is possible to compare the utilities of individuals of different generations by attributing to their utilities either the same weight or different weights (normally, decreasing importance is given to future generations as time is extended forwards). It becomes evident that, if the same weight is attributed to the utilities of individuals belonging to different generations, then the solution is substantially identical to that adopted by Pigou in a different context.

9.5 PURE COMPETITION AND PARETO OPTIMALITY

One of the main results of economic analysis is that of having proved that, *if pure competition prevails in an economy, a position of Pareto optimum is automatically reached.* In more technical terms: *every competitive equilibrium is a Pareto optimum.* This concept can also be expressed as follows: if the goods and the factors of production (capital and labour) are produced and exchanged in conditions of pure competition, then the resources (i.e., the factors of production) are used *efficiently* (that is, economically or rationally), and production reaches its maximum.

The idea that an organisation of the economy based on pure competition leads to the maximum advantage for all the individuals can be traced back to the end of the Eighteenth century in the work of the founder of economic science, Adam Smith. The same idea is expressed more or less explicitly by many later economists, until Pareto's contribution.

The reasons why a situation of maximum advantage is believed to occur in competition are manifold. In the first place, *in competition the price of goods tends to be equal to their cost of production.* Let us assume that for farming the cost of production of one pound of potatoes is of twenty pence; this cost includes rental fees for land, expenses for growing the potatoes and transporting them to the market. Let us further assume that farmers sell potatoes for twenty five pence a pound. They therefore make a large profit (five pence per pound). At this point other farmers would want to replace their vegetable and grain crops with the more profitable potato crops. The result would be an increase in potato crops, which, in turn, would cause their price to fall. Over an extended period of time the price of potatoes would drop to twenty pence, i.e., to the cost of production.

Another consideration is that *competition creates a situation where production is oriented by consumers.* If consumers want potatoes, farmers will grow potatoes; if consumers want carrots, farmers will grow carrots. For the farmers it is of no importance whether they grow potatoes or carrots, and thus they adapt their crops to the consumers wishes.

Finally, *competition* forces firms to use the factors of production (capital and labour) efficiently (i.e., economically or rationally) and *forces the economy to reach the maximum possible volume of production (of goods and services).*

This can be seen from the following example. Let us assume that a product can be manufactured by two different techniques, one of which uses more capital and less labour than the other. For instance, a certain number of garments can be produced either by using complex machinery (requiring high capital investment) and little labour, or simple machinery (requiring a small capital investment) and a greater number of workers. Now let us consider the reasons for adopting one technique rather than the other.

For each investment good (or machinery) there is a certain demand and supply; the same holds true for labour, as there are workers who offer their skills and firms who look for workers to hire. The price of each piece of machinery is determined by the equilibrium of supply and demand; in the same way the price of labour, that is the wage level, is determined by the equilibrium between the supply and demand for labour. In an economy in which machinery is abundant (that is, the supply of machinery is greater than its demand) and labour is scarce (the demand for labour from firms is greater than its supply), the price of machinery is low while wages are high. This situation leads firms to adopt production techniques which are highly mechanised, that is, which require a great deal of capital and little labour. This occurs in highly industrialised countries such as the United States or Germany. On the other hand, in many underdeveloped countries machinery is scarce and labour is overabundant. In this case the opposite occurs and firms adopt techniques which are relatively non mechanised.

Thus we can deduce that since the price of each good (or factor of production) is determined by the equilibrium between its supply and demand, in practice prices reflect and actually measure the relative scarcities of goods (factors). If a good is scarce (demand is greater than supply), its price is high. If a good is abundant (supply is greater than demand), its price is low.

Thus we can see that the prices of productive resources (goods and factors), in so far as they measure their *relative scarcities*, guarantee an efficient (that is, economic or rational) use of these resources, because firms use scarce resources with greater parsimony and abundant ones with less. In this way, the waste of resources is avoided, and a maximum level of production is reached, thus obtaining a Pareto optimum.

However these considerations apply only where pure competition exists, because this is the only case where the prices of productive resources reflect their relative scarcities. For instance, an abundant resource can have a high price if its supply is controlled by a monopolist or by a few oligopolists.

9.6 THE EQUIVALENCE OF PURE COMPETITION AND PARETO OPTIMALITY: THE IMPLICATIONS FOR ECONOMIC POLICY

The basis of the idea (which was already implicit in Adam Smith's analysis) that pure competition allows the highest possible level of production led economists throughout the last century to maintain that the state should not intervene in the economy because it would cause production to fall, resulting in the destruction of wealth. Therefore, economic activity was to be left to the initiative of each individual (firms, consumers, workers, etc.), according to the principles of free enterprise or *laissez-faire*.

It was held that the state should limit its intervention to three types of action: to guarantee the conditions of competition, avoiding the formation of monopolies; to guarantee certain essential services such as military defence, the administration of justice etc.; to modify, if necessary, income distribution.

In our analysis on Pareto optimum, we noticed that the maximum production level can be reached even when the distribution of income is very unfair. For example, in a country where investment goods are scarce and the population is overabundant, market forces make wages very low. In this situation there is an efficient use of resources but an unfair distribution of income. Therefore the state, on the basis of a political decision (the decision cannot be scientific since a comparison of the utilities of different individuals is not scientifically possible), can intervene to change the distribution of income.

At a later stage, economists began to consider the possibility of state intervention in other areas, mainly because they thought that *in pure competition prices could diverge from the costs of production, given that so called social costs occur. These represent a cost for the community but not for firms*. We shall return to this point later.

Various authors have stressed that free competition does not always allow consumer sovereignity. Firms, and especially large ones, can influence consumer tastes through advertising. Furthermore, the demand for goods depends on individual incomes, that is, on the distribution of income among individuals. For instance, in an economy where there are only a few wealthy individuals and a lot of poor ones, there is a demand for (and therefore the production of) a limited number of luxury items and a large quantity of basic goods (primarily food). On the other hand, in an economy in which the bulk of the population lies in the middle class, with an income which is neither excessively high or low, there is a large demand for secondary goods (beverages, household appliances, cars, television sets) and firms produce these goods. Consequently, consumers do not rule the market, because the distribution of income has a great influence on demand and therefore on the production of goods. The state must therefore intervene both to regulate advertising and to influence the distribution of income among individuals, taxing the rich and subsidising the poor.

Another problem is that free competition does not always allow the maximum level of production. Keynes, back in 1936, showed that the full utilization of resources is not always automatically achieved; rather, there is a tendency for the economy to stagnate with unemployed workers and unused machinery. Thus it becomes necessary for the state to intervene in order to ensure full employment. However, as we have seen, this point is object of much debate and controversy.

State intervention is also contemplated in the area of international trade. Some economists admit that the state can, in certain circumstances, protect national industry by subsidising it or by imposing duties on imported goods. We shall examine this topic later on.

9.7 THE DIVERGENCE BETWEEN PRIVATE COSTS AND SOCIAL COSTS; MARKET FAILURE

The equivalence between pure competition and the optimum for the community was based on Adam Smith's idea that, if every individual pursued his private interest (consumers try to obtain the maximum utility, entrepreneurs the highest level of profit, and so on), the maximum advantage for all individuals, that is, the maximum social advantage would be attained. However, this is not always the case, because even in a situation of pure competition, there are differences between *private* and *collective* or *'social' interests*.

This phenomenon, first touched upon by the British economists Marshall and Sidgwick, was thoroughly analysed by Pigou, who showed that it is not unusual for *private* and *social costs* to diverge. For instance, a factory producing chemical products that pollute the air and the water of a nearby river with its waste products does not include such factors in its costs. However, these damages represent a cost for the community. In this case, social costs are greater than private ones. An investment consisting of the creation of such a factory generates an *external diseconomy*, i.e. a *negative* or *detrimental externality* which is outside the factory but within the economy.

Pigou also gives some opposite examples. In an underdeveloped country the construction of a railway extending from the interior to the coast, although providing a very small benefit for the company that builds it because the traffic is small, provides an incentive for the creation of industrial activities inland, by making it possible to transport products to the coast. In this case, the *social advantage* (that is, the advantage for the community) that derives from the construction of the railway is greater than the immediate *private advantage* for the company that builds it. In this case the construction of the railway generates an *external economy*, i.e. external to the investing company, but internal to the economy (a so called *positive* or *beneficial externality*).

In these situations, which occur even in pure competition, the state must intervene: in the first case to penalise the polluting factory with a tax which makes it pay for its social costs; in the second one to create an incentive in the form of a subsidy which reduces the costs of building the railway.

Some authors maintain that in many cases it is not enough to tax the firms or the individuals who damage the community and repair the damage with tax revenue, but rather that there should be voluntary or coercive regulations to limit or to avoid the damage. For instance, the unregulated use of private cars within the historical centres of cities can create a situation in which the flow of traffic is completely paralysed; motorists and citizens might want to agree to limit private traffic, either on a voluntary basis or by state or locally enforced regulations. We can imagine many situations of this kind in which, by itself, the market

131

cannot bring about results which are socially advantageous, thus making public intervention necessary. In these cases, we speak of a *market failure*.

Other authors stress the fact that the state, just as it should try to reduce social costs, or at least have them covered by those who are responsible for their production, must also try to create beneficial externalities aimed at improving economic development. For instance, in a developing country or in an underdeveloped area of an industrial country, a certain investment, like the construction of a dyke which would make a river navigable, by itself does not give a sufficient profit and therefore no private enterprise would want to carry it out. Nonetheless, it would create other opportunities for investment and profit for industries which produce boats and sporting equipment or swim wear, given that, once the river becomes navigable, it can be exploited for commercial or touristic purposes. Thus it may be advisable that the state builds the dyke.

In conclusion, the state should generally intervene to make a firm or an individual causing a social cost pay for it; in some cases it should directly regulate certain phenomena (for example, traffic); furthermore, it should subsidise those activities which give a greater advantage from the social rather than from the private point of view or even assume the responsability of promoting and running such activities.

Several authors have criticised these conclusions, maintaining that public intervention to correct external effects is costly because it results in an increase in bureaucracy and in an excessive interference in business decisions that discourage private entrepreneurship. The English economist R.H. Coase stresses that the cost of the provisions to remove externalities must also be considered, and that the phenomena must be evaluated under all points of view. An example given by Coase is that of a hypothetical industrial plant which discharges toxic fumes causing damage evaluated at one hundred dollars: it might seem advisable, at first, to have the owners of the plant pay a one hundred dollars tax with which the damage can be repaired; moreover, if it was possible to install a filter which costs less than one hundred dollars and eliminates the emission of fumes the firm would profit by doing so. But this solution might not be the best one for the community, if those affected by the fumes could be moved from the contaminated area for a cost of sixty dollars. This second solution would make the community save forty dollars.

Coase and other authors maintain that the problem of externalities arises also because property rights are not well defined. For instance, a firm can pollute a private garden or a river (which belongs to the public) without paying any compensation. It would be therefore necessary to carefully define and regulate property rights.

Coase and others further maintain that the problem of externalities could in general be solved through agreements between the parties involved (in our example, the owners of the polluting plant and the individuals affected by pollution). The parties could agree some compensation for damages, thus making public intervention and the connected bureaucratic costs superfluous. To hinder this type of spontaneous agreement between litigants amounts to interfering in property rights and subsequently to weakening them.

Other authors (Binmore, Farrell, etc.) have shown however that there are very few cases in which spontaneous agreements might really solve the problem of externalities, because the cost of these agreements could be so high that it is extremely unlikely that they would ever be achieved, and therefore public intervention remains necessary.

Among those who are not in favour of public intervention we can also mention the exponents of the *theory of public choice* (Buchanan, Tullock and others), who point out first of all to the fact that politicians pursue objectives which are different from public interests, such as power in itself, ideology, clientship; and secondly that bureaucracy tends to develop as a centre of power. For these reasons it is always preferable to seek solutions of a contractual nature, that is spontaneous agreements between the victims of damage and those responsible for it.

In line with this reasoning we also find the theorists of supply side economics, who favour deregulation, i.e. the reduction of public regulation of private economic activity (for example building industry, transport, work environment, health, etc.), because they maintain that public intervention, with its inevitably sluggish bureaucracy, discourages private enterprise, reducing productivity and the economy's growth possibilities.

In any case, what remains unresolved is the conflict between those who maintain that the amount of social costs which is unpaid (by those who have created them) is enormous (ranging from costs in human terms like job accidents to pollution, to the destruction and uncontrolled consumption of natural resources) and therefore corrective public intervention is essential, and those who reject public intervention because they consider it incapable of regulating the complex question of social costs efficiently.

The observation that the divergence between private and social costs is a widespread phenomenon has led economists to formulate *cost-benefit analysis*. The latter is used by politicians, even if only partially, in decision-making regarding public investment. This type of analysis considers, with reference to an investment project (for example the construction of a road or an airport), both the private benefits and costs deriving from the assets and liabilities of the investing firm, and the social costs and benefits, i.e. the costs and benefits that the project produces for the community (for example, for the construction of an airport, the social cost of air and noise pollution, which is measured in terms of either the cost for the inhabitants in the area to move away or the devaluation of real estate in the area). A public investment project is undertaken only if social benefits are greater than social costs. In practice, social benefits and costs are not easily measured, and this is one reason why cost-benefit analysis constitutes only one out of many elements upon which public decisions concerning investment are based.

The field of cost-benefit analysis also embraces the techniques for evaluating the impact on the environment. These aim at measuring the effects caused by an investment project on environmental resources. The use of this technique is becoming ever more widespread, in part because many countries tend to create laws which limit pollution.

In the context of the preceding analysis, the problem of the *cost of economic development* arises. This concerns the external diseconomies generated by growing industrialisation, urbanisation and congestion. In recent years there has been the development of a new position which calls for limiting growth since its supporters maintain that an excessively rapid growth of production damages the environment, the quality of life and risks exhausting the natural resources of the planet. Here we can cite the uncontrolled consumption of primary sources of energy, the destruction of the last remaining forests like those of the Amazon, etc. . On the other hand, however, it is noted that the problems of congestion and pollution of industrial countries are much less serious than those of underdeveloped ones, where there is an urgent need for rapid development enabling the population to raise their extremely low standard of living.

Furthermore, history has shown that economic resources are quite different from physical ones. Technical progress has often provided synthetic alternatives to natural resources as primary materials (plastic has replaced wood on a large scale, synthetic fibres have replaced wool and silk, nuclear and aeolian energy has replaced oil, etc.); technical progress has also raised the productivity of natural resources: the use of chemical fertilisers and biotechnology has greatly increased the productivity of land, so that the production of foodstuffs in the last twenty years has increased enormously throughout the world. The total depletion of the natural resources of our planet therefore does not seem to be a realistic perspective.[1]

Continuing our analysis of market failure and the consequent need for public intervention, one category of goods on which economists have concentrated their attention is that of *public goods*.

For example, the historical centre of a town is an instance of a 'common good', but analogous problems arise with 'public goods', such as a lighthouse on a cliff. In this case, there is no problem about voluntary limitation or regulation in the use of the good (as is the case of the historical centre), because all ships that pass by (whatever their number) can see the lighthouse (that is, they can use the service) and thus avoid crashing into the cliff. However, market mechanisms do not allow for the payment of such services by those who use them (ships), nor can they exclude those who refuse to pay (the so called *free-riders*) from the use of such services. Thus, no private individual or enterprise would find it advantageous to produce this type of good, and state intervention becomes necessary to produce it: this is both a case of divergence between private and social interests, and another example of market failure. As early as the nineteenth century, the British economist Sidgwick had pointed out that no private individual or firm would profit from building a lighthouse on a cliff. Therefore all ships would crash into the rocks and there would be a reduction in national wealth; thus, the need for state intervention to construct lighthouses.

Moreover, there are cases in which not all individuals have perfect information; for instance, the level of information is much greater for the seller than for the consumer. For example, a doctor who sells his services to a patient is much more expert than the latter about the problems of diagnosis and therapy; the same applies to a mechanic who repairs his customer's car. The less informed individual (the customer) has to trust

135

the provider of the service (the doctor or the mechanic) as he does not know how to choose him. In all these cases (*contracts with incomplete and asymmetrical information*), individual action does not allow to reach an optimum; either a general agreement or state intervention is necessary, which ties individual action (in the example, that of the doctor or the mechanic) to a moral code of behaviour which is richer than the code of merchant morality mentioned by A. Smith. What is required is a Kantian code of professional ethics, otherwise the pursuit of personal profit on behalf of each individual fails to lead to a Pareto optimum.

9.8 ECONOMIC SCIENCE AND MORAL PHILOSOPHY

Some authors have considered the problem of a purely competitive market in the more general context of the functioning of social life. Under this heading we find the *neo-institutionalist* school, with its two branches: the *neo-Austrian* or *evolutionist* and the *contractualist* approaches.

Neo-institutionalism developed at the University of Chicago and counts among its exponents both jurists and economists. They maintain that the relations among economic subjects in modern capitalist societies are regulated by a complex set of norms which concern the rights of property, the use of public goods, contractual relations among subjects, etc. . Neo-institutionalists study these relations to evaluate whether they originate from inadequacies in market mechanisms. In other words, externalities, public goods, etc. are all 'market failures', i.e. situations in which the market is unable to lead to a position of optimum for the community and it thus becomes necessary for the state to intervene. Nevertheless the type of intervention required is not limited to taxation and subsidisation as suggested by Pigou, but consists of the creation of an adequate series of norms and institutions.

The Austrian economist Hayek, and his American colleague Nozick are among the authors who uphold the neo-Austrian or evolutionist school. They maintain that free interaction between individuals produces rules of behaviour and institutional mechanisms which create political order and economic progress. Such political order and economic progress is generated by the free interaction which takes place among individuals and not by a project which they consciously adopt and pursue.

Others authors, like Hurwicz and Buchanan, who represent the contractualist line of thinking, base their analysis on the idea that individuals can organise their social life according to a conscious plan. They must create an economic-institutional organisation which is adequate for a society of free individuals. The problem is that of agreeing upon an optimal political constitution for the society, i.e. a series of rules agreed upon in advance and which everyone must respect.

Other approaches have reconsidered the problem of the choices that a community must make, i.e. social choices, as elaborated by the economists -and in particular by Arrow- who attempted to construct a social welfare function. The Indian economist Sen criticises the method of constructing a social welfare function together with the entire conceptual apparatus of welfare economics. According to Sen, in constructing a social welfare function it is not enough to use individual preferences as a basis, and especially the preferences of all the individuals. He grounds his reasoning not only on the fact that the preferences of certain individuals are undoubtedly antisocial but also on the fact there are certain inalienable rights, which must be respected even if they are not desired: for example, freedom of the press, freedom of expression, etc. which some individuals, having always lived under an oppressive regime, might not even desire. Thus, in the construction of a social welfare function, it is necessary to take into consideration not only the preferences of the individuals but also the principles of ethics. Sen's considerations make the problem of constructing a social welfare function even more complex and reinforce Arrow's conclusion that it is impossible to do so.

All the theories examined so far, from Pareto onwards, reach the conclusion that economic science cannot indicate criteria of distributive justice. The possibility of maintaining that a given distribution of income is more or less just with respect to another is not an economic question, but one of moral and political philosophy. These conclusions, which consider economics as a neutral science, as Robbins defined it, have led in recent years to strong criticism and to a growing interest in the topic of *distributive justice*. The aim is to formulate a scheme of reference within which to consider simultaneously both the problems of efficiency and those of justice (or equity). Among the theories which have dealt with these topics, the most famous one is that elaborated by the American philosopher Rawls, according to whom all social values (freedom, job and career opportunities, income and wealth) must be distributed equally among all individuals, unless an unequal distribution of some (or all) of these values results in an advantage for all the members of the community, or at least for those who are in the worst conditions. In other words, for Rawls, the only inequalities which are acceptable are those which improve the position of the poorest members of the community. If, for instance, a greater inequality of income causes higher saving and investment and this situation in turn creates a rise in wages for the lowest paid workers, then this type of inequality can be accepted.

Hayek and Nozick take a different stand from Rawls'. According to them, the criteria for justice must not be limited to evaluating the 'final state' of a process of distribution (for Rawls, for example, a more unequal distribution is preferable if it ensures that the income of all individuals is higher and especially the one of the individuals who had the lowest salaries), but rather the institutions must be judged independently of the final results they produce. For instance, if everybody agrees that a competitive market is a good institution, then the result produced by competition must be considered just.

This approach, which relies mainly on the role of individual initiative, has been criticised by authors like Sen, who have studied the problems of inequality and poverty especially in developing countries, and who have shown how market mechanisms fail to guarantee a distribution of income which is ethically acceptable.

While the British economist Atkinson and others have tried to elaborate statistical indexes which measure the inequality of income and poverty, basing their work on long standing Italian and French studies, others have carried out research on the psychological attitudes of individuals regarding the problems of inequality and poverty. Some authors have shown that many individuals who are wealthy or comfortably off are in favour of programmes for redistributing income in favour of the less well off. Thus, the traditional microeconomic position according to which each individual maximises his own utility, which in turn depends solely on the commodities he consumes, is not realistic, since individuals are also capable of *philanthropic behaviour*. This means that the utility of an individual depends not only on his own consumption but also on the consumption of other individuals: in other words, the utilities of different individuals are not independent but interdependent. In the same way the utility of an individual can depend on public programmes aimed at helping the less well off and at transferring income to them.

Just as philanthropic behaviour exists, so does behaviour determined by envy, exhibitionism, etc. . An individual might suffer, in the sense of having a decrease in his utility, because consumption of other individuals increases while his own remains stationary or grows too. All of these types of behaviour violate the principle of Pareto optimum, which assumes the independence of individuals' utilities. Several authors have however redefined the concept of optimum taking into account the interdependence of utilities of individuals and especially philanthropic behaviour.

9.9 THE GROWTH OF STATE INTERVENTION IN THE ECONOMY

State intervention in the economy has increased enormously especially since the Second World War. Many countries have pursued a policy aimed at *redistributing income* from the most wealthy to the poorest social groups through progressive taxation of incomes and the creation of pension systems, subsidies and free or low cost social services (medical care, rent controlled housing, etc.) for the poor. Just how well these policies have achieved the desired effect is a controversial point. There is no doubt that the living conditions of the large majority of people in industrial countries have greatly improved over the last few decades, but this has come about mainly as a result of the increase in the production of goods and services rather than because of a process of redistribution of income.

Studies carried out on monopolies have shown that the formation of large enterprises allows for a notable reduction in production costs; this phenomenon is connected to the concentration of technical and financial forces which have developed over the last hundred years. Thus it is neither realistic nor advisable for the state to reestablish a competitive situation in all sectors. On the contrary, it is better to acknowledge the existence of large firms so that the community does not lose the advantages mentioned above, while at the same time making sure that large enterprises are not allowed to take advantage of their positions. In many countries, this objective has been achieved through the creation of an *antitrust law*.

Following *Keynes' analysis*, it has been held furthermore that in an economy ruled by free competition, full utilisation of the available resources is not automatically achieved; for this reason, special forms of state intervention are necessary, ranging from monetary and fiscal policies to incomes and prices policies.

Other types of intervention that we have considered concern education, urban planning, industrial policy and in general all those measures which favour development and diminish its human costs, for example subsidising declining sectors (like agriculture or certain types of industry) and favouring a gradual movement of workers from these sectors to the expanding ones. The state can intervene in the economy to direct investment and development by controlling banks and firms, for instance through nationalisation.

One area in which state intervention has greatly increased in the last few decades is that of *social security*. In many countries there has been a tendency to make insurance compulsory for workers to cover certain risks (accident, illness, unemployment) and to substitute insurance companies with direct action on behalf of the state, through the creation of special structures. Thus in many countries it is the state which provides for pensions (retirement and disability) and free or low cost medical care. The opposite tendency – that against an excessive growth of the welfare state – has not substantially modified its foundations, nor does it seem likely to be long lasting.

The state can also intervene in the field of *international trade*. Following the Second World War, a notable liberalisation in trade among industrial countries has taken place, but not between these and developing ones. In particular, industrial countries continued to protect their agriculture, and even today measures of industrial protectionism as well as laws for controlling and limiting the movement of capital and people are applied. Protectionist policies have been pursued by the majority of underdeveloped countries.

A large part of state intervention in the economy, as we have seen, is aimed at promoting development. Many economists have pointed out that the equivalence between pure competition and Pareto optimum remains correct in a *static framework*, in spite of all the limitations we have examined. As we have seen, if we consider an expanding economy and examine it over a fairly long period of time, we also have to take into account the preferences of the individuals who are not yet born.

140

Furthermore, in the theorem of the equivalence of pure competition and Pareto optimum, the prices of goods determined by the market are considered in a given moment, but there is no examination of the way in which they vary over time.

In recent years several economists have tried to examine the problems of the efficient use of resources in a *dynamic framework*, together with that of a definition of some type of criterion for an optimum (other than Pareto's which, for the reasons we have seen, is not applicable to a dynamic economy), but the results which have been reached to date are quite limited.

9.10 THEORY AND MODELS OF ECONOMIC POLICY

The need to coordinate measures of economic policy within a coherent framework is the basis for the analysis elaborated by the Norwegian economist R. Frisch and his Dutch colleague J. Tinbergen, which aims at providing a *rational basis* for economic policy, that is to elaborate a 'theory of economic policy'. These authors discuss Bergson's concept of the social welfare function and point out that, since it is not possible at a practical level to build up this function by taking into account the preferences of all the individuals, it must be considered as the *politicians' scale of preferences*. Frisch and Tinbergen try to elaborate a logical scheme into which the *objectives* that politicians aim to achieve and the tools available to them can be inserted, in order to evaluate the adequacy of the latter with respect to the former. This type of procedure would eliminate the risk that those responsible for economic policy make decisions based exclusively on intuition, experience and the ability to predict future needs.

This logical scheme, expressed in a mathematical form, is referred to as a *model of economic policy* or as a *planning model* and it provides the means for making coherent decisions. Essentially, a model includes the economic policy objectives or targets (for example, a given level of consumption, of employment, etc.) and the available tools (for example, monetary policy, fiscal policy, manoeuvers concerning the rate of exchange, etc.) which represent the means available to the authorities for reaching the targets.

Experience has shown however that the implementation of these models, that has been done in various countries, cannot substitute completely economic policy which consists of day to day action of public authorities, aimed at mediating and harmonising the interests and requests of different social groups.

Following the logic of these models, Tinbergen maintains that the politicians' preference function must be built up by economists, who should interview politicians in order to understand their aims and objectives. However, as Tinbergen points out, in elaborating politicians' preference function, economists must not limit themselves to setting down acritically politicians aims, because economic analysis should formulate suggestions about these aims, in order to eliminate any possible incompatibility among various aims; it should also take into account new facts or aspirations, define more clearly those goals which the politicians have indicated in a vague way, provide ways of interpreting long standing goals in more modern terms; and create new ones where necessary. And, as Tinbergen adds, in dealing with the problem of goals, economic analysis must reflect a political attitude aimed at satisfying general interest on a world scale, at reducing the income gap between rich and poor nations, and considering any modifications of institutions which might be deemed necessary to reach these goals. Economic analysis therefore is not confined to a merely passive function of accepting the goals which have been established externally (that is, by politicians), but it must also actively clarify and critically evaluate existing situations and be prepared to solicit innovation. As we have seen, this view is quite distant from Robbins' concept of the neutrality of economic science and it is close to Keynes' view, which was not limited to advising an increase in public spending in order to reach full employment, but called for radical changes in the preexisting economic institutions, for example, to transform the stock exchange into something different from the gambling casino that it was or to create a more equal distribution of income among different social groups and among different parts of the world.

In the same way that Tinbergen distinguishes among *quantitative policy* (for example, a variation in tax rates), *qualitative policy* (which is deeper, as for example the introduction of a new tax) and *reform policy* (which determines a change in the institutional bases of the economy, like the introduction of a programme of social security), so have German economists always distinguished between *Ordnungspolitik* and

142

Prozesspolitik, in which they define the former as the economic policy concerning the institutional framework (which can therefore be modified) and the latter as the policy concerning economic processes, i.e. aimed at reaching objectives within the existing institutional framework. Economists are authorized to concern themselves also with reform policy, that is with *Ordnungspolitik.*

While on the one hand the work of Tinbergen has been carried on by Theil, on the other a relevant contribution to the 'theory of economic policy' was given by the British economist Meade, who defines the objectives of contemporary economic policy as full employment, the most economically efficient use of resources and a distribution of income in line with the wishes of the community. Meade does not set up the objectives by interpreting the wishes of politicians, but rather by deducing them from the historical awareness one has of their relevance, that is by the spirit of the times (for example, everyone or nearly everyone today considers full employment one of the main objectives of economic policy, as Ricardo at his times considered the maximisation of the rate of accumulation the most important goal to be achieved).

Keeping in mind that the ideas of Frisch, Tinbergen and Meade were formulated in the Fifties and the Sixties, we can see that the rediscovery of the ethical dimension of economics in opposition to Robbins' idea of the neutrality of economic science, applied in the Seventies and Eighties by authors like Rawls and Sen, reflects a continuity of ideas with the preceding authors.

9.11 ECONOMETRICS AND EXPERIMENTAL ECONOMICS

From the Thirties onwards there has been an intense development of *econometrics*, a discipline which aims to use mathematical analysis to formulate a relation between economic variables and statistical analysis in order to specify the functional form of these relations and to estimate them. For example, consumption increases when income increases; econometricians try to determine in precise mathematical terms the laws which link increases in consumption with increases in income in a given country in a given period. The purpose is to formulate predictions about the future trend of economic variables. If we know the exact law which links consumption to income, we can forecast that, if in the next years income will increase by a given amount, then consumption will also increase by a given amount.

Econometricians have refined their techniques in such a way as to build models to forecast the future trend of the economy's main variables (consumption, investment, prices, employment, etc.) as well as the effects of economic policy measures on these variables (for example, the variation in a tax rate, an increase in the quantity of money, etc.). In the language of the models of economic policy of the type formulated by Frisch and Tinbergen, it is thus possible to forecast the effects that the use of any tool produces on the objectives. Very rarely however do such predictions turn out to be exact, due to the fact that events can occur and there can be changes in the behaviour of individuals which are difficult or impossible to foresee.

Furthermore, over the last few years studies in *experimental economics* have been developing and attracting a growing interest. This field of economics carries out research on the micro-economic behaviour of individuals, recreating in a laboratory environment situations which are analogous to those dealt with in real life. By observing directly the decisions made by participants in experiments, researchers aim to test the validity of hypotheses and conclusions of economic theory. Individuals taking part in the experiments act and are required to make decisions in conditions which simulate reality, thus allowing researchers to observe their behaviour.

One fairly famous example of this type of analysis is the experiment carried out in 1969 by two researchers, K. Mac Crimmon and M. Todo, which involved a group of students. The experiment aimed to study the preferences of consumers and their characteristics. The subjects were asked to choose among various combinations of a pair of goods (money and sweets), where each combination contained a varying quantity of the two goods. In this way the researchers were able to verify for instance that the participants always preferred a combination which contained a larger quantity of both money and sweets to one which contained a lesser quantity of each.

9.12 THE THEORY OF ECONOMIC PLANNING

The considerations made up to now concern *market economies*, that is those economies in which the means of production may be privately owned, the organisation of firms is basically free, the prices of goods are set by producers, and the distribution of income among the different social groups is not set by planning authorities but rather depends on the behaviour of firms, workers and the organisations which express their positions collectively (business associations, workers' unions), as well as on the measures taken by public authorities.

On the other hand, in countries with a *planned economy* (USSR, other East European countries, etc.) the means of production, with very few exceptions, are publicly owned. Decisions regarding what goods should be produced and in what quantities, what production techniques are to be adopted, etc. are taken by central planning bodies and the prices of goods are also set by these bodies.

One of the main problems arising in planned economies is how to achieve an *efficient use of resources*. In market economies, as we have seen, the price of each commodity (or production factor), in so far as it is determined by the equilibrium between supply and demand of the commodity (or factor), reflects its scarcity. This occurs only in pure competition, where prices ensure an efficient or rational use of resources, forcing firms to use scarce resources more sparingly than abundant ones.

In planned economies, since prices are fixed by planning authorities, there is no automatic mechanism to guarantee the efficient use of resources. If, however, planning authorities want resources to be used efficiently, then they must attribute to goods and factors those prices which would be determined automatically in a purely competitive economy as the result of the working of market forces (supply and demand).

This result, discovered by the Italian economist E. Barone in 1908, is the basis of the theory of planning, developed by economists both in the East and the West. It is the reciprocal of the previously examined theorem, in which a situation of pure competition equals a position of Pareto optimum. What we are affirming here is that, if a planned economy wants to reach a Pareto optimum, it must fix the same prices for goods and factors that would be determined by market forces in a purely competitive economy. In a planned economy, these prices should be

145

calculated mathematically by the central planning bodies and they are referred to as *shadow prices* or *efficiency prices*.

The calculation of shadow prices for the economy of a country is not yet a feasible operation, in spite of extensive developments in the field of cybernetics and the use of computers in recent years. This type of calculation, in fact, requires the formulation and solution of an enormous number of equations within a very brief period of time.

In the Soviet Union and in the other main socialist countries central authorities, being unable to calculate shadow prices, set up production goals expressed in quantitative terms. Factories are asked to produce a given number of shirts, television sets, automobiles, and if possible to overfulfill the planned targets. Among the main defects of the system, which are also recognised by economists of socialist countries, is that the increase in quantity usually comes to the detriment of quality and that the use of resources is not efficient.

Nor can these inconveniences be ignored with the excuse, given for example by the British economist Dobb, that a planned economy has as its main aim that of development, whereas the problem of efficiency regards a static situation. As we have already illustrated, even in an expanding economy the problem of the efficient use of resources exists, even though it cannot be considered in terms of the equivalence of pure competition and Pareto optimum. Studies carried out regarding *dynamic efficiency* and its possible equivalence with a situation of pure competition have not yet reached a conclusive stage.

In order to avoid, or at least to reduce, the above mentioned and other inconveniences, various Eastern economists have proposed to introduce a certain degree of decentralisation in decision making, allowing individual factories to decide, within certain limits, what production techniques they want to adopt, which goods to produce and their quantity. This suggestion, which was first elaborated at a theoretical level by the Polish economist O. Lange in 1936 would allow for at least a partial recreation of a market. The result of this reform would be that the supply and demand of investment goods would determine their prices and these in turn, by reflecting the relative scarcity of goods, would guarantee a rational use of productive resources. In this way, while public ownership of the means of production would remain, mechanisms which are typical of a market economy would be reintroduced into a planned one. It is not surprising that this type of proposal has so far been met with strong resistance at the political and ideological level in socialist countries.

Due to the current rapid changes taking place in East European countries, it is not yet possible to forecast what the evolution of these economies will be. It is too early to guess if in the next few years economists will have to study a completely new problem, like that of the transition from socialism to capitalism, while to date only the transition from capitalism to socialism has been studied.

Another important problem for planned economies is that of *plan coherency*. Let us suppose that the plan (worked out by central authorities) foresees for the year 1992 the production of 80 trucks, 40 tractors, 30 washing machines and 30 pounds of steel. If 30 pounds of steel are not sufficient to produce the given quantities of trucks, tractors and washing machines, the plan is incoherent.

In general, in order to produce a given quantity of any final item (for example, a certain number of trucks), the quantities of intermediate goods (iron, glass, rubber) need to be determined. Thus, the plan should make sure that the quantities of intermediate goods available, whether produced nationally or imported, is the same as those needed to produce the final goods. For instance, the plan must foresee that the quantity of wood produced is exactly the same as that required by all the factories using wood in manufacturing (factories producing furniture, doors, prefabricated houses, etc.).

In countries with a planned economy, the problem of plan coherence is solved by using the *method of material balances*. For each intermediary product (wood, for example) a list is made which expresses the availability of that product (i.e., the quantity of that item which has been produced) and another one is drawn up for the sectors where the item is needed. For every (intermediary) item, the accounts must balance, i.e. the quantity produced (or imported) must be sufficient to supply what is to be used.

The method of material balances, developed in the Twenties in the Soviet Union, was perfected by the American economist W. Leontief, who at the end of the Thirties created the *input-output analysis*.

It is not easy to draw up an account for all the goods produced by an economy, partly because one would have to know the technological and marketing structure of the whole economy. For example, one would have to know how much iron is required for the production of one truck, one tractor, etc. . The quantity of one commodity (iron, for example) which is required for the production of a unit of another commodity (an automobile, for instance) is referred to as *technical coefficient* or *production coefficient*. The set of technical coefficients of the economy make the *input-output matrix* (or *table*) or Leontief's matrix.

NOTES

1. Even in the Nineteenth century the British economist Malthus theorised that population was increasing more rapidly than available resources, and he consequently foresaw a progressive reduction in the standard of living of the population. Theories which foresee the total depletion of the planet's natural resources are consequently called *neo-Malthusian*. However, Malthus' predictions have to date been widely disproven: the world population has greatly increased, but so has its living standard.

10 The theory of value and distribution

10.1 RECENT DEVELOPMENTS IN THE THEORY OF GENERAL ECONOMIC EQUILIBRIUM

As we have already seen in the chapter on neoclassical microeconomics, one of the main conclusions of neoclassical theory and general equilibrium theory is that, for all goods, prices are determined by the interaction of demand and supply, and therefore also by consumers' tastes and preferences, which, in turn, determine demand. The conclusion does not change once money is introduced in the general equilibrium scheme. In fact, as many authors have pointed out, in neoclassical theory money affects the general level of prices, but not relative prices, as we have already seen. In the last fourty years many contributions on the theory of general economic equilibrium have been developed, most of which, however, leave its basic conclusions unaltered.

In this respect, the first problem economists have addressed is whether a set of equilibrium prices *exists*, i.e. if there is a set of prices that simultaneously makes demand and supply equal for each product. Given that equilibrium prices exist in practice, economists had to show that even in (mathematical) general economic equilibrium models such prices exist and that they are significant in an economic sense, i.e. that they are not negative.

Another problem can be summarised as follows: assume that market prices are not at their equilibrium level, i.e. that they do not equate demand and supply. Then, does the economy have automatic forces that bring market prices to their equilibrium level, i.e. that equate demand and supply for each good? The problem is that of the *stability* of equilibrium. If the answer is yes, the system is stable, otherwise it is unstable.

Recently other economists have questioned the general equilibrium method maintaining the importance of analysing *disequilibrium* instead. For instance, so far analysis has been based on the assumption that, when the price of a product is too high and some of it remains unsold (i.e. supply is higher than demand), sellers offer a lower price. In turn, this determines a reduction of supply and an increase in demand, and the price continues to fall until demand and supply become equal. To simplify the mathematics of the process, economists assumed that no exchange takes place at prices other than equilibrium ones, i.e. that any exchange is actually made only when prices are such that demand and supply are equal. This was Walras' original assumption, which he named *tâtonnement*, giving the main idea of groping in the dark.

Recently many economists have abandoned this assumption, in favour of the more realistic one that exchange takes place even at non-equilibrium prices. However, if this is the case, it seems extremely unlikely that the economy converges to equilibrium, i.e. that prices can assume values that equate demand and supply. In such an instance, instability appears to be the rule, and stability the exception.

Other economists have pointed out that the *lack of information* on the state of the market can push sellers and buyers to follow a *perverse* behaviour: for instance, it could prevent sellers from lowering their prices even when supply exceeds demand. Similar results can be obtained by considering *expectations*. For instance, if enterprises expect the demand for the goods they sell to increase in the near future, they will not lower their prices, not even if part of their goods are unsold – if, in other terms, there is an excess supply. In this case the economy does not tend automatically to equilibrium.

Some economists (Clower, Leijonhufvud and others) underlined that Keynes dealt particularly with the problems raised by the lack of information and the role of expectations. It was precisely with reference to these problems that Keynes denied the existence of an automatic mechanism bringing the economy to its full employment equilibrium. According to Keynes, the equilibrium mechanism does not rely on price variations, but on quantity variations, as we have seen in the chapter on Keynesian economics. However, even in an economy where equilibrium is ensured by variations of production rather than of prices, there are problems due to the lack of information and the role of expectations. An enterprise experiencing a rise in the demand for its goods would not hire more labour to raise supply if the increase in demand is seen to be purely temporary. These ideas led many economists to the conclusion (which, in part, is implicit in Keynes' thought) that it is essential for the state not to limit its intervention merely to making some investment, but to also act as a *coordination and planning centre*. State intervention would thus be relevant even for private agents, and this is all the more important given that the lack of information and of certainty prevents market forces from bringing the economy to its full employment equilibrium. Economists supporting the free market such as M. Friedman and R. Lucas have a completely different idea. They view the market as being basically stable and as having in itself regulating forces which, if not perfect, are in any case better than state intervention, given that the latter, in general, ends up by increasing instability.

10.2 THE REVIVAL AND FURTHER DEVELOPMENTS OF THE CLASSICAL THEORY OF VALUE

Neoclassical general equilibrium analysis is: (i) limited to the short run, and (ii) considers essentially the exchange of goods. When production is analysed, it is considered to be marginal with respect to exchange. In such a framework, the price of goods is determined by demand and supply. The demand for goods is, in turn, determined by consumers' preferences. It has therefore been maintained that in neoclassical economics and in particular in general equilibrium theory prices are determined at a *subjective level*, given that they depend on agents' preferences. Moreover, given that prices are determined by the equilibrium between demand and supply, they reflect the scarcity of goods, as we have already seen.

This approach, that is called *neoclassical* or *marginalistic*, emerged around 1870. The classical economists (Smith, Ricardo and Marx) had a

151

different theory on the determination of prices, the so called labour theory of value, according to which the value of a commodity is given by the quantity of labour necessary, both directly and indirectly, to produce it, i.e. by the quantity of labour contained in the good.

Any commodity (for instance, wheat) is produced by means of labour and of machinery (hoes, sickles, or tractors). In turn, machinery and tools are produced by means of labour and other machinery. In other words, capital is *always* produced by means of labour and capital. Therefore, for classical economists, the only original factor of production is labour, whereas capital is only 'frozen labour'.

In the long run price tends to equate value for each good.

This theory has at least two difficulties. The first one is that, from a logical point of view, it is not possible to add up quantities of labour of different periods, or quantities of labour of a different quality (for instance that of an unqualified worker with that of a qualified one, or that of an engineer, and so on). The second obstacle derives from the fact that goods are produced also using factors that are not entirely identifiable with labour: for instance land in agriculture, and raw materials, i.e. natural resources, that are scarce and are not frozen labour. However, classical economists did not consider these points, which they thought to be unimportant.

The labour theory of value leads to results that are completely different from those of neoclassical theory. The prices of goods, in fact, are determined by the quantities of labour they contain rather than by demand and supply. Given that individual preferences (that is, subjective preferences) have no influence on prices, it is maintained that these are determined at an *objective level*.[1]

Demand can influence the price of a good only in the short run. An increase in demand makes the price rise with respect to its value, while a reduction makes the price fall. In the long run, however, the prices of goods tend to be equal to their values.

As they are not determined by demand and supply, 'objective prices' do not reflect the scarcity of goods. The amount of labour necessary (both directly and indirectly) to produce a good is determined by current technology. For instance, technical progress reduces the amount of labour necessary to produce a good and therefore lowers its price.

According to some economists and to some scholars in the history of economic thought, the difference between neoclassical and classical theory depends essentially on the fact that the first considers the short run and the second the long run.

In the short run, it is maintained that exchange is the dominant phenomenon, so that prices are determined by demand and supply and therefore by subjective preferences; in the long run, however, it is the technical conditions of production that determine prices. However, one should not forget that, living in the Eighteenth and Nineteenth century, classical economists had in mind a society where salaries were very low, barely enough to guarantee survival, and most individuals could not really choose between various consumption goods. The rise of people's standards of living that took place in the last decades of the Nineteenth century led neoclassical economists to consider the consumer's problem in terms of a choice between different goods.

Starting in the Sixties some authors – in particular Piero Sraffa – reconsidered the classical theory of value, opposing the marginalistic approach according to which prices are determined at the subjective level. Sraffa, however, does not consider labour to be the only original factor of production, but underlines how every commodity is produced by means of other commodities. For Sraffa the process of production is not a one way process leading from factors to final commodities, because even these, in turn, are used to produce factors. For instance, iron is necessary to produce tools and machinery, but, to extract it from the mines, iron tools are needed. Similarly, wood is necessary to produce an axe, which, in turn, must be used to cut trees and to produce wood. Production, in other words, is not a one way but rather a *circular process*.

In this, Sraffa's approach differs basically from the neoclassical theory of production. As we have seen, neoclassical analysis is essentially limited to exchange. When production is taken into account, it is generally considered as a one way process, based on a strong distinction between the final product and factors (capital, labour, land). According to neoclassical economists, the amount of production depends on the amount of factors used, while the problem of how factors themselves are produced is not considered.[2]

According to Sraffa, a commodity can enter directly into the production of another commodity (for instance, the axe into the production of wood), as well as indirectly (for instance, into the production of a table: it serves to produce wood, which, in turn, is needed for the table).

153

Sraffa distinguishes all commodities into two categories: basic and non basic. The first enters either directly or indirectly into the production of all commodities, while the second does not. For instance, iron is a basic commodity inasmuch as it is necessary for the production of many goods, which in turn are necessary for the production of many other goods, and so on. Even a lorry can be a basic commodity, given that it is used for transport (and therefore enters into the production) of many commodities, which in turn enter into the production of other commodities, and so on. The same can be said of wheat, or bread, that feed both animals and humans, whose labour enters into the production of all commodities. On the other hand a necklace, a bracelet and in general all luxuries are non basic commodities.

According to Sraffa a commodity's price is given by the sum of the quantities of commodities that are needed for its production, each multiplied by its price. However, as this occurs for each commodity, it is not possible to determine the price of one good independently from that of the others, so that all prices are determined *simultaneously*. The prices thus obtained depend on the technical conditions of production: demand, and therefore consumers' preferences, play no role.

Some authors have associated Sraffa's framework to the theories of price determination based on the costs of production. These, being based on an empirical observation of reality, maintain that, when fixing the price of goods, enterprises do not consider (present or future) demand, but the costs of production (measured in monetary terms). For instance, an enterprise producing refrigerators would calculate the cost of production of each unit by aggregating costs for raw materials, wages paid to workers, fixed costs for machinery (divided in proportion) and so on. The price of a refrigerator would be calculated by adding a markup to this cost.

Apart from any empirical consideration about whether enterprises really behave as described, i.e. if they actually ignore demand, this theory differs considerably from that of Sraffa. In fact, it still views production as a one way process leading from factors to the final product, while one of the main aspects of Sraffa's analysis is that there is no difference between factors and final goods, and that *commodities are produced by means of commodities*. In the theories based on the costs of production, instead, the problem of how all prices are determined simultaneously is not even posed.

According to Sraffa, labour too can be considered a commodity that is produced by means of other commodities. Workers, in fact, eat bread and meat, dress with clothes, shoes and so on. Therefore 'labour' is 'produced' by means of these goods (bread, meat, clothes, shoes, and so on), which, in turn, are obtained by means of other commodities (wheat, animal fodder, machinery to produce clothes) and so on.

In a slave economy, or in a system like the one during the first phase of capitalism, wages consist of the quantities of consumption goods necessary to guarantee the survival of workers, as classical economists maintained. However, this is no longer the case, and it is unrealistic to assume that labour's price, i.e. wages, is determined in the same manner as the price of any other commodity, that is by the amount of commodities necessary for workers survival. Sraffa considers present reality, even if he fails to answer the main question: what forces determine wages? This raises the question of the distribution of national income between profits and wages, which will be dealt with in the following paragraphs.

10.3 GENERAL EQUILIBRIUM ANALYSIS AND THE THEORY OF ECONOMIC GROWTH

As we have seen, general equilibrium analysis originates as a static theory explaining the determination of equilibrium prices in a given moment or in the short run. However, in the last thirty years, many economists have tried to 'dynamise' this theory, by considering not only exchange but also production. Among these contributions are those 'models of economic growth' that are based not on the analysis of a small number of macroeconomic variables (income, investment, profits and so on) as we have seen in chapter seven, but rather on a framework in which there are n (where n is a very large number) consumers, n firms and so on.

These models, the most important of which are those by J. von Neumann and by Morishima, deal essentially with production in a growing economy and consider the dynamics (i.e. growth) of the economy in a framework similar to that of classical economists and their followers, such as Joan Robinson (see chapter seven). Some of these models, however, also account for exchange, and others are closer to the neoclassical theory of growth, inasmuch as they assume that wages and interest rates are flexible and that firms can change the technology they use (for instance, they can employ relatively more labour and less capital). These models, that are of a multisectoral rather than of a macroeconomic nature, focus on *balanced growth*, in which all the economy's sectors grow at the same rate, so that relative proportions remain unchanged. Even though this assumption is unrealistic, departure from it complicates the models from the mathematical point of view, which explains why unbalanced growth has not been extensively investigated. One exception, in the sense of a model in which the size of each sector changes with time relative to the others, is that proposed by the Italian economist Pasinetti.

In an attempt to apply the criterion of Pareto optimality to a dynamic economy, balanced growth models have been analysed from the point of view of their dynamic efficiency. As we have seen, however, this leads to great difficulties.

10.4 THE MAIN THEORIES OF DISTRIBUTION

The goods produced in the whole economy (i.e. national income) are distributed among the agents that take part in production. If, as a simplification, only two categories of agents (workers and firms) are considered, one must see how national income is distribued among them, that is, how it is distributed between wages and profits.[3]

For *classical economists*, wages are at the subsistence level. The latter is determined not by purely biological needs, but by historical and social factors. Profits are a *residual income*, determined by the difference between national product and wages. For Ricardo there is a further category of income, i.e. rent, originating from land. However, as agriculture has progressively lost its importance in the economy, due to the industrial revolution, the two main categories of income remain wages and profits.

Neoclassical theory changes the theory of distribution dramatically by introducing the *principle of scarcity* in the markets of the factors of production. Wages are determined by the equilibrium between the (firms') demand for labour and the (workers') supply of labour. If demand is higher than supply (i.e. labour is scarce), wages are high. On the other hand, if labour supply is abundant with respect to demand, wages are low.[4] Given that income produced is distributed between capital and labour, what really matters is relative scarcities. Therefore, if labour is abundant with respect to capital, wages are low and profits are high. The opposite happens if labour is scarce. The first case occurs, for instance, in a country like India, the second in one like the United States.

In the last thirty years many economists have strongly criticised this theory. Their criticism largely relates to the concept of capital implicit in neoclassical theory. With reference to classical theory, it is in fact maintained that capital is not an original factor of production, but rather it is 'frozen labour'. Moreover, Sraffa has shown that, if every commodity – or at least every basic good – enters (directly or indirectly) into the production of every other commodity, it is not possible to distinguish products from factors (apart from labour, for the reasons we have already mentioned). Therefore, the notion of capital as something different from final goods has no meaning, and more important still, there is no criteria by which the 'scarcity' of capital can be measured. However Sraffa, although criticising neoclassical theory, does not provide his own theory of distribution. On the other hand, today the classical hypothesis of wages being at the subsistence level appears unacceptable.

Kaldor has developed a 'neo-Keynesian' theory of distribution which differs from both the classical and the neoclassical one. In part, Kaldor's contribution was anticipated by various authors, such as Keynes and Kalecki. According to Kaldor, modern economies operate in conditions that are close to full employment, as governments tend to adopt Keynesian policies to support demand. Under such circumstances a rise in demand determines not an expansion of production, but an increase in prices of goods (in the short term), which, in turn, given that firms produce and sell goods, implies an increase in their profits. Firms decide the amount of investment; an increase in investment determines, through the Keynesian multiplier, an expansion in total demand. Given that the economy is in full employment, this does not produce an expansion of production, but an increase in prices and thus in profits.

In this framework wages become a residual income. In fact, the level of investment determines prices and profits. Given that the volume of national income in terms of the physical quantity of production is fixed (it cannot rise, since the economy is in full employment), the level of wages is determined as the difference between national income and profits.

Other theories, however, (like that of Kalecki) point out that firms operating under monopolistic or oligopolistic conditions have much larger profits than firms operating in competition. Therefore, the higher the firms' *degree of monopoly*, the larger the share of national income going to profits and, consequently, the less that going to wages.

Nowadays, the labour market in industrial countries is characterised by *collective bargaining* between employers' associations and trade unions. This is a situation of *bilateral monopoly*, in which the result, i.e. the level of wages, is determined essentially by the relative strength of the two sides.

Moreover, in various countries there are firms operating in an oligopolistic regime which can, within certain limits, raise the prices of the products they sell, while others cannot do so because they operate in a situation close to competition. There are also workers who benefit from a monopolistic position in the bargaining process with firms, because they are organised into trade unions. Therefore these workers can get higher wages, while others, who are not organised, do not have this power. In such a situation it is not uncommon that, as we have seen, firms operating in an oligopolistic regime grant wage increases to organised workers in order to reduce conflict in the firm; at the same time, they make up for the higher costs by raising the prices of the products they sell. This reduces the purchasing power for those groups who do not benefit from any increase in their monetary incomes while prices are rising.

Both the firms and the groups of workers who have monopolistic power take larger and larger shares of national income, to the detriment of firms and workers operating in competition. Often the situation is worsened by the introduction of mechanisms that index wages (see chapter six), which in practice cannot be extended to all groups of workers.

10.5 MODERN THEORIES OF ENTERPRISE BEHAVIOUR

One of the main shortcomings in the theories of price determination reviewed so far concerns the fact that they do not consider the complexity of the behaviour of enterprises. Modern enterprises are complex organisations, and one must consider their structure and behaviour, which have not been fully accounted for by the analyses described so far.

Starting in the Thirties economists stressed the fact that one of the features of large enterprises is the *division of its ownership*. This is seen best in a corporation, which is an entity different from its owners, so that none of the single shareholders is responsible for the management of the company or for its debts.

A modern industrial firm has two other important features: *the separation of ownership from control* and *the diversification of products*.

The first phenomenon derives from the division of ownership and consists of the fact that shareholders have a very limited possibility of determining the corporation's possible options, given that the main decisions relative to investment, price determination, wages, etc. are taken by managers. In principle, managers should carry out the general policies set by the board of directors, elected by the meeting of shareholders, but in practice managers tend to be largely independent and have strong personal initiative powers, thanks to their stronger competence and experience compared to the members of the board of directors. Therefore, large firms are *de facto* directed (that is controlled) by persons other than the owners.

The other characteristic of industrial firms is product diversification. Large firms frequently do not produce a single commodity, but a variety. They invest in different sectors according to the convenience of the moment and market perspectives. In such a way by investing in the sectors that tend to have the highest profitability, they seek to maximise overall profits. Product diversification reduces the risk of losses, given that, when a certain sector undergoes a crisis, a 'diversified firm' operating in a variety of fields suffers fewer losses than one that has invested entirely in one sector, which can go bankrupt.

On the basis of these considerations, the British economist Marris, together with others, has noted that modern industrial enterprises do not strive to maximise profits, but rather to *expand in size* as quickly as possible, investing in various sectors. The success of managers is measured on the basis of their ability to increase the size of their enterprises. However, there is a constraint to this: by striving to expand, enterprises could always reinvest their profits, without distributing them to shareholders as dividends. In such circumstances, the *market value of the firm* and thus the demand for its shares could fall, which could make the enterprise unable to find funds to finance growth, its main target.

Other authors have emphasised that an enterprise growing too rapidly undergoes a short run reduction of profits, given that financing new investment and acquiring new markets is costly. Moreover, if the interests of managers lead to maximising the growth of the enterprise, the interests of shareholders, which managers must take into account, concern the market value (i.e. the stock exchange value) of shares. This interest derives from the fact that shareholders selling their shares earn an amount close to their market value, and also from the fact that an extremely low stock exchange value of shares can encourage a takeover on behalf of individuals external to the firm. A firm's behaviour should thus reflect the twofold interest of managers, the expansion of the firm, and of shareholders, an increase in the market value of shares.

These contributions capture an important aspect of modern industrial enterprises, which has been further analysed by the American economist Simon, who, with others, has created the so-called behavioural theory of the firm. Modern enterprises are not individual units, as traditional theory postulates. Rather, they are organisations, i.e. they include a number of people and decision makers (managers, workers, shareholders, customers, and so on) each pursuing a particular objective. Managers, for instance, pursue the target of enterprise expansion, which can give them power, prestige and higher salaries; workers strive for high wages and good working conditions; shareholders would like to have high dividends and a high share value, and so on. The behaviour of a firm thus results from the interaction of all these choices. A large firm, therefore, is not a subject (like a manager or a small enterprise could be), but a complex organisation whose activity cannot be fully planned and controlled by managers. In fact, even if managers take the ultimate decisions concerning the firm's activity, these in turn depend on the information they receive and on the actions of many other agents.

Alongside this framework other economists (the so called neoinstitutionalists, like Coase and Williamson) underline the fact that complex, hierarchically structured and organised firms are created precisely because they reduce costs with respect to atomistic firms operating in competitive markets. Moreover, modern industrial enterprises do not adapt passively to the market structure and to the existing technological conditions. Rather, they influence the external environment by following strategies aimed at increasing their market power.

160

Recently various authors have formulated the *theory of contestable markets*. Such a market, for instance that of cars, is characterised by the presence of few firms, as in an oligopoly, but also by the fact that other enterprises may enter the market easily, i.e. without costs.

Returning to the example of cars, it is true that production in this field requires considerable financial means and a great deal of technical expertise, so that an individual or a small firm cannot, in general, start producing cars. However an enterprise e.g. already producing aeroplanes could do so without facing excessive costs.

Therefore, an enterprise can enter a contestable market; it does so if it expects to make profits by selling production at a price equal to or lower than that fixed by the existing firms.If the enterprise entering the sector sells its production (for instance, cars) at the same price as the other firms, it does so only if it thinks that demand for that good is not entirely met; otherwise, it sells the good at a lower price in an attempt to attract some customers (i.e. a share of demand) from the enterprises already in the market.

Naturally, it can always happen that, when the new enterprise enters the market, those already there react by lowering their prices. In fact, if they have high profits, they can easily do so.

Finally, other authors have focused their attention on *multinational corporations*, i.e. on those companies that act and have plants in different countries. The first firms of this type were created at the beginning of this century, but it is only since the Second World War that they have become widespread. The reasons why companies become multinationals are manifold, and amount to risk curtailment, the possibility of exploiting other countries' favourable conditions like low cost manpower, low taxes, among others.

One of the advantages of multinational companies is the diffusion of technology and of modern forms of organisation to all countries. Governments, however, and especially those of small countries, distrust these companies, given that they can easily move their capital from one state to another. This enables them to have a strong effect on a country's economy and its domestic policies, for instance by creating unemployment when they leave.

NOTES

1. This point can be understood by means of a simple example by A. Smith. In a primitive economy, agents live by hunting deers and beavers. A hunter needs two hours to find and kill a deer and only one to find and kill a beaver. The amount of labour necessary to produce a deer is therefore double than for a beaver. The exchange necessarily takes place at the price of one deer for two beavers.

    Assume that an agent has hunted and killed some deers, and tries to sell them on the market in order to obtain more than two beavers for each deer, for instance three beavers. No one is willing to pay such a price, because it takes three hours to kill three beavers, while it takes only two hours to kill a deer. Anyone who wanted to buy a deer prefers to hunt it himself. Therefore, whoever wants to sell a deer must accept no more than two beavers in exchange.

    In such an instance, whatever are individual preferences and hence the demand for deers and beavers, the price is always of one deer for two beavers (that is one beaver for half a deer), i.e. it is determined uniquely by the amount of labour necessary to produce the goods (two hours for one deer, and one hour for one beaver). Individual preferences, and therefore the demand for deers and beavers, determine only the quantities supplied – for instance, if agents prefer deers to beavers, deers are hunted more – but they have no influence on their prices.

    This result, however, is based on a number of restrictive hypotheses. If the model is complicated, even the results change.
2. According to some neoclassical economists, like the Swedish economist Wicksell, labour, land and raw materials are 'original factors', while fixed capital (plant and machinery) is 'produced' by means of labour and other factors. These economists however, unlike the classics or Sraffa, did not consider all the consequences of this statement.
3. To be more accurate, however, one should distinguish between categories of income and categories of people. In fact, profits and wages do not necessarily coincide respectively with capitalists' and workers' incomes. For instance, in a country like the United States, where the ownership of shares is fairly common, a worker can have an income made in part by his wage and in part by profits (i.e. by dividends on his shares).

    This distinction has become more and more relevant as workers have started to earn wages that are high enough to allow some savings, with which they can acquire bonds and shares, which give capital income, i.e. profits. However, the problem that is dealt with in this chapter concerns the distribution of national income between categories of income and not of people, i.e. the *functional* rather than the *personal* distribution of income.
4. The idea of scarcity, however, was, to some extent, relevant also for classical economists. In fact, they thought that the wage level was determined by the demand and the supply of labour, but that it tended to gravitate to the subsistence level, as foreseen by *Malthus' Law of Population*, according to which the population tends to grow more rapidly than production. For Malthus, every

time wages rise, workers have more children. This makes the population grow, labour supply increase and wages eventually diminish returning at the subsistence level.

For Marx, however, wages remain around the subsistence level due to the presence of the *industrial reserve army*. When there are unemployed workers in an economy, the supply of labour is bigger than demand, and therefore wages are low, at the subsistence level. As a consequence, profits are high and this encourages capitalists to invest and to expand production, thus gradually reducing unemployment. When full employment is achieved, labour demand becomes higher than supply and wages increase. This reduces capitalists' profits, who therefore curtail investments and labour demand. Unemployment – which Marx calls the industrial reserve army – is created again and consequently wages tend to fall at the subsistence level.

11 International economic relations

11.1 THE THEORY OF COMPARATIVE ADVANTAGE AND ITS MODERN DEVELOPMENTS

From the days of the classical economists, the problems of international trade have been analysed separately from those relating to the exchange of goods within a country. For many reasons international trade does not obey the same rules of internal trade.

For instance, the *mobility of the factors of production* (capital and labour), although high within a country, is much lower between countries. Even if there has been and indeed still is intense migration and capital movements among states, this phenomenon is less relevant with respect to factor mobility within a country. The same can be said of *technology*, which spreads within a country much quicker than between different countries.

These elements, along with each country's *different endowments* of natural factors such as climate, fertility of land and raw materials, make production of certain goods cheaper in one country while others are cheaper in another.

In the Thirties the theory of *comparative costs* (or of *comparative advantage*) was still dominant. The first version of it was given by Ricardo, and was further refined, among the others, by Marshall, Edgeworth, Taussig and Viner. Let us consider two goods and two countries, which, in Ricardo's example, are respectively cloth and wine, Britain and Portugal. Assuming that production of both goods is possible in each country, but the production of cloth is cheaper in Britain and wine is cheaper in Portugal, it would therefore be appropriate for Britain to specialise in the production of cloth and import wine, and for Portugal to specialise in the production of wine and import cloth.

So far, the theory may appear obvious. What Ricardo stressed, however, was that in determining specialisation among countries it is not the *absolute advantage* that a country has in the production of a good, but the *comparative advantage*. Let us suppose that Portugal has an advantage in the production of both goods (that is, it produces both cloth and wine at a lower cost than Britain), but the advantage is not uniform with regard to both goods, being greater for wine. For instance, the cost of producing a yard of cloth is 90 man hours (labour hours) in Britain and 70 hours in Portugal, while the cost of one gallon of wine is 120 hours in the former and 70 in the latter. In these circumstances Portugal should specialise in the production of wine and import cloth.

Let us assume that the pay for an hour's work is equal to one pound in both countries. Portugal, by exporting a gallon of wine, costing 70 hours of labour, can receive in exchange up to 119 pounds (this is because Britain finds it convenient to import wine while the price per gallon remains below 120 pounds). With 119 pounds Portugal may import from Britain more than one yard of cloth (paying 90 pounds per yard, or perhaps a little more). If Portugal had made cloth herself, 70 man hours would have produced one yard of cloth. Instead, thanks to international trade, with 70 man hours, by producing and exporting a gallon of wine, she gets a yard of cloth and some to spare.

It is evident in this example that trade is convenient for both countries and therefore it takes place.[1] The fact that international trade occurs even when a country has an advantage in the production of both goods, but a greater advantage in one good rather than the other, has been called the *Ricardian paradox*.

Ricardo's theory and its developments analyse how the *international terms of trade* are determined, that is how the ratio between the prices at which the two goods are traded on international markets is fixed.

However it has been pointed out that to determine the convenience of trading between countries the *costs of transporting* goods across the borders must also be taken into account.

As we have seen from the example, Ricardo measured the costs of producing goods in terms of labour hours; according to classical theory the value of a good is given by the amount of labour necessary to produce it. With the neoclassical approach, the prices of goods are not determined by the amounts of labour they contain, but by individual preferences, and the theory of comparative costs was reformulated.

In particular, Haberler measured the costs of production of goods not in terms of hours of labour but in terms of *opportunity cost*. If, for instance, by using all its available resources, an economy produces 100 pounds of bread and 80 of meat, and if to produce one additional pound of bread it has to reduce the production of meat by half a pound, the opportunity cost of bread (in terms of meat) is half a pound. The opportunity cost, in other words, indicates the alternative production which one must give up in order to obtain an additional unit of a given good.

Haberler's contribution introduces the theory of comparative costs into the marginalist framework and hence, by taking into account many goods and many countries (instead of only two), into the general economic equilibrium framework. The basic results of Ricardo's theory, however, are left untouched.

In the last few decades many authors have tried to *test empirically* the theory of comparative costs. Basically, what they have done is to compare the exports of certain goods of two different countries towards other markets, where transport costs and barriers to trade are roughly the same for both countries. Assuming that the cost differences between the two countries are determined by the differences in labour costs (which are given by the ratio between labour productivity and the wage level), the country with the lowest labour costs should export more to third countries than the other. In practice, the results of these empirical tests appear to confirm the theory of comparative costs. However, as it often happens with empirical tests, results can give rise to different interpretations, so that the debate on the subject is not yet closed.

11.2 THE THEORY OF HECKSCHER AND OHLIN

We have seen that international trade originates from differences in the (comparative) costs of production of goods among countries. One of the prime causes of such differences is the different endowments of productive factors among countries, which is determined not only by different endowments of natural resources, but also by a country's stage of development, by its social institutions, in a word, by its history.

For instance, India is relatively more abundant in labour than capital (plant, machinery, etc.), while the opposite occurs in the United States. The Swedish economists Heckscher and Ohlin maintain that each country tends to export those goods whose production requires a *more intense usage* (that is, contains a larger amount) of the factor with which it is relatively more richly endowed. Therefore, countries like India tend to specialise in the production of goods that contain labour rather than capital, i.e. goods with a low technology content, produced with simple machinery, like shoes, textiles, and so on. Countries like the United States, on the contrary, specialise in the production of goods that require a more intense use of capital, i.e. goods with a high technology content, like electronics, products of the nuclear industry and so on. Each country, therefore, exports the goods in whose production it specialises.

Empirical tests, however, have not always confirmed this theory. While, for instance, India does export goods with a high content of labour and imports goods with a high content of capital, just as envisaged by Heckscher and Ohlin, the United States also exports labour intensive goods, even if it is specialised labour, and imports goods with a high capital content. This result, that contradicts the theory of Heckscher and Ohlin, is named the *Leontief paradox*, after the economist who first expounded it. In the Sixties Japan, which was definitely overendowed with population, exported capital intensive goods and imported labour-intensive ones.

Heckscher and Ohlin, moreover, maintain that the *prices of the factors of production* in the countries engaging in international trade *tend to equalise*. This point has been studied particularly by the American economist Samuelson. As a country that is overabundant in labour specialises in the production of labour intensive goods, the firms demand for this factor grows, and so do domestic wages. The demand for capital, in turn, stagnates and consequently its price tends to fall. A country that is overabundant in capital specialises in the production of capital intensive goods, and therefore does not produce labour intensive goods, the demand of capital grows and that of labour falls, so that the price of capital tends to increase and wages tend to fall.

When factors such as capital and labour are mobile (even if only partially) across countries, the tendency of their prices to equalise should be even stronger.

Experience, however, does not confirm this theory. In countries where capital is abundant there is normally a rapid technological progress. This determines a rise in labour productivity, which, in turn, leads to an increase in wages. However, this does not occur in countries where the population is relatively abundant in relation to capital (as it is the case of less developed countries).

Certainly, restrictions on free trade and on the free movement of factors could be an element that limits the tendency to equalise factor prices among different countries. However such a tendency comes into action slowly and only in the long run, because there are many elements which counteract it.

11.3 THE THEORY OF THE PRODUCT CYCLE

The debate on the theory of Heckscher and Ohlin shows that international trade cannot derive solely from the different endowment of factors of production in each country. It is essential to take other elements into account, especially technological progress. Considering such a framework, *the product cycle theory* aims at classifying the stages of life of a product, in order to derive some conclusion on the composition of international trade and its evolution.

A new product always requires research, experimentation, adaptation and possibly modifications. This, in turn, is based on the intensive use of specialised labour, high costs of production, and therefore the product is sold at a high price. This is the *introductory stage* of its life.

Later comes the *stage of development*, during which the product is mass produced and distributed on a large scale. The importance of labour in the production process declines, while the intensity of capital increases. The number of producers grows, while the cost of production falls and supply increases. As a result, the price of the product falls.

As the market approaches saturation, the *stage of maturity* comes. The volume of sales of the product touches a limit, even if some firms can raise their market share by reducing that of others. In this stage, the product is completely standardised and the production process relies even more intensely on capital. Production units become bigger and the labour force is essentially non-specialised. At this stage a price rise would cause a strong fall in demand.

As we have seen, this theory aims at explaining the composition and the evolution of international trade. In the past, the introduction of new products has been most frequent in countries with a high level of income per head, like the United States where cars and electrical household appliances were common before other countries. When goods are in their development stage, they spread to the countries that have a lower income per head. For instance, in Western Europe cars and electrical household appliances have become mass produced three decades after than in the United States. When goods enter the maturity stage, they spread to countries that presently are underdeveloped. For instance two centuries ago textiles were produced in Britain, while now they are largely produced in underdeveloped countries.

This theory places great emphasis on technology and its changes to explain international trade flows.

A different theory has been put forward by Helpman and Krugman, who maintain that each country sells abroad goods at a price which differs from the internal one. They suggest that each country tries to take advantage of the structure of demand of every other country and this determines the current flows of international trade.

11.4 PROTECTIONISM AND FREE TRADE

Ricardo and his followers maintain that international trade is convenient whenever there is a difference in the comparative costs of countries. These studies, therefore, underline the benefits of the international division of labour and of policies that ensure free trade.

However, countries have often adopted *protectionist policies*, aimed at reducing imports and increasing exports. The main instruments of these policies are *customs duties* (or *tariffs*), *import quotas* and *subsidies to national industry*.

While duties are taxes affecting foreign goods entering the national territory, quotas consist of the maximum quantity of foreign products that are allowed to be imported.

Subsidies (or premiums) are granted by a government to firms, and may be either grants, tax reductions, or low cost credits to exporting firms. We shall see that the same results may be obtained by adopting currency regulation policies.

Duties and subsidies alter the prices of goods and hence also comparative advantage, reducing international trade. Quotas achieve this objective directly. Protectionist policies curtail the advantages of production specialisation underlined by the theory of comparative costs, and thus reduce wealth.

However the factors that cause countries to adopt protectionist policies are many and varied. The first is not strictly economic: a high degree of specialisation can reduce a country's political independence, if it then becomes dependent on foreign trade for strategic supplies like foodstuffs or military equipment.

Other arguments in favour of protectionism are of an economic nature. Some authors maintain that protectionism in favour of a given industry could allow internal output to grow and thus expand employment. The most well known argument is that of the *infant industry*, by which a country must protect its industry from external competition in its initial stage of development, in order to strengthen it. Protectionism, however, should be abandoned once the industry becomes strong. Another argument is that of *employment*: duties increase production and, consequently, employment in the protected sectors.

Several economists have considered what could be the *optimal tariff structure* for a state, implicitly assuming that free trade does not necessarily represent the best choice for a single country. In particular, the following problem can be considered by means of an example: if the United States puts a duty on Italian shoe imports, and Italian producers cannot sell shoes elsewhere, they will lower the price in order to sell the same quantities of shoes to the United States. In this case the duty does not protect the American shoe industry effectively, but has a purely fiscal nature. The situation is the same as if the United States applied a tax on Italian shoe producers, given that the duty falls on foreigners.

It is evident however that *a priori* nothing forces us to think that foreigners (in this instance Italian shoe producers) will pay the duty. If the United States does not have the monopoly of the demand for Italian shoes, producers can sell them elsewhere and thus will not reduce prices. Thus foreigners agree to pay the duty only under certain conditions.

In the past, the degree of protectionism has varied according to

170

different circumstances. The only exception being Britain, who was the first nation to experience an industrial revolution and therefore had no competitors in international markets, all other countries had to protect their newly created industries from foreign competition.

In the period from the first half of the nineteenth century to the First World War free trade prevailed, even if it was occasionally interrupted by periods of protectionism. One of these occurred after 1880, when states like Italy and Germany wanted to protect their newly created industries, while European countries also sought to protect their national agriculture, given that the advent of steam ships and railways allowed the United States and Argentina to export large quantities of wheat to Europe at low prices.

Protectionism prevailed strongly between the two world wars. In the Thirties nationalist policies led to more protectionism, to bilateral trade (i.e. to the attempt, on behalf of each country, to have a balance of trade with every other single nation in equilibrium[2]), and finally to *autarchy*, that is the tendency for each country to produce domestically all the goods it needs.

After the Second World War the non socialist countries undertook to abandon bilateralism and to return to free trade. They aimed at creating a general system of economic, monetary and commercial relations between countries with a market economy, managed by special organisations like the *International Monetary Fund*(IMF) and the *International Bank for Reconstruction and Development* (IBRD), created in 1944 by the Bretton Woods agreements.

To gradually reduce duties, quotas and export premiums and to coordinate tariff policies among members, the *General Agreement on Tariffs and Trade* (GATT) was created in 1947, by means of an agreement reached by twenty three countries. These countries now number more than one hundred. Within GATT various conferences have been organised, like the *Kennedy Round*, the *United Nations Conference on Trade and Development* (UNCTAD), the *Tokyo* and the *Uruguay Rounds*.

The first round, named after the then President of the United States, was held in Geneva from 1964 to 1967. It was aimed at reducing customs barriers between Europe and the United States, but it largely missed the target. UNCTAD held two sessions, one in Geneva in 1964 and another one in New Delhi in 1968, aimed at increasing trade between industrial and developing countries particularly in favour of the latters exports of agricultural products and raw materials. However industrial countries have continued to protect their agriculture and there has been little improvement in the liberalisation of trade. Therefore, trade between non-homogeneous countries (that is, between industrial and developing ones) has remained stagnant, while it has grown considerably within the industrial world. This is also due to a number of agreements, the most important of which created the European Economic Community in 1957. The EEC has gradually eliminated all obstacles among members to the free circulation of human beings, goods and finally capital, it has created a common external tariff for third countries and has adopted a common policy for agriculture and transport.

Even the Tokyo Round (opened in Tokyo in 1973 and closed in Geneva in 1979) and the Uruguay Round, opened in 1986, have had only a limited success in the liberalisation of trade.

Finally, there are other protectionist instruments, that differ from the 'classic' ones already considered. These are called *non tariff* barriers and consist of all the obstacles to trade other than tariffs. Non tariff barriers are extremely widespread and have developed rapidly especially since the mid Seventies. They represent a way of overcoming international agreements like GATT that envisage a reduction of world protectionism by curtailing duties and import quotas. Many countries, like the United States, Japan and others have reduced duties and quotas, while introducing various non-tariff barriers.

Two instances of non-tariff barriers are *voluntary export restraints* and *health regulations*.

Voluntary export restraints consist in country A using its political strength to convince country B to reduce its exports to A. For instance, in the Eighties the United States persuaded Japan to reduce its exports of cars to the United States, by stating that, if Japan did not voluntarily reduce its sales of cars to the United States, they would impose duties not only on Japanese cars, but also on other Japanese products. Moreover, the United States would have reduced their military contribution to the defence of Japan. The Japanese Government released a smaller number of export licences to firms exporting cars to the United States and thus reduced its exports to that country.

Another example is given by health regulations. Mexico produces excellent fruit, but the United States does not allow its importation because it is not produced according to the US health rules. Mexican agricultural firms could produce fruit according to these rules, but this would raise their costs. Therefore, the situation is the same as if the U.S. had imposed a duty on Mexican fruit.

11.5 THE GOLD STANDARD AND KEYNESIAN THEORY

The *gold standard* was the mechanism regulating international economic relations from 1870 up until the First World War. Each country declared its currency's *parity* with respect to gold and agreed to *convert* it into gold on the basis of this parity to whoever wanted it. If for instance the parity of Germany's currency was one mark for 1/4 ounce gold, anyone taking a one mark note to the central bank of Germany would have received 1/4 ounce of gold and vice versa.

This meant that central banks had to keep enough gold reserves to convert all the notes in circulation, or at least the largest part of them, according to demand and on the basis of the official parity. Consequently, the amount of money in circulation in a country was *proportional* to the gold stock owned by the central bank. In fact, when the latter received gold, it gave notes in exchange, and when it received notes it gave gold. Therefore, an increase (reduction) in a central bank's gold reserves would determine an increase (reduction) in the amount of money in circulation.

In this system the exchange rate between two currencies[3] is, in practice, equal to the ratio between the parities of the two currencies with respect to gold. If for instance one lira was equal to one ounce of gold and one pound was equal to two ounces of gold, the exchange between pound and lira would be one pound to two liras. If agents in the currency market asked for three liras for one pound, anyone wanting to buy pounds with liras would go to the Bank of Italy, from which, giving two liras, he would obtain two ounces of gold. These, in turn, could be sent to the Bank of England to get a pound in exchange.

In this case, a pound would cost two liras plus transport and insurance costs of gold. From this example, one can see that the exchange rate between two currencies can differ from the ratio between their gold parities by only a small amount determined by transport and insurance costs. Therefore, the exchange rate is *fixed*.

A country with a balance of payments deficit, due for instance to an excess of imports over exports,[4] pays for this difference by an outflow of the national currency; foreign agents then ask the central bank of the deficit country to convert it into gold. Therefore, countries with balance of payments deficit have an outflow of gold, while those with a surplus have an inflow of gold. As we have seen, this produces a reduction in the money in circulation in the first group of countries and an increase of the money in circulation in the second group. Consequently, according to the quantity theory of money, prices diminish in deficit countries and rise in surplus ones. On international markets, the goods produced by the surplus countries become less competitive and therefore their exports fall. The opposite occurs in deficit countries, whose exports rise.

Therefore, the gold standard grants an *automatic mechanism* that brings balances of payments in equilibrium.

A Keynesian extension to the analysis of balance of payments adjustment states that the latter does not take place uniquely by means of price variations, but rather because of variations in income and employment. In fact, if the economies do not have full employment, surplus countries registering inflows of gold and therefore increases in the amount of currency in circulation, experience an increased demand for goods and services and consequently an increase in income and employment. The increase of aggregate demand and of people's incomes leads to an expansion in the demand for foreign goods, i.e. for imports. On the other hand, in deficit countries the amount of money in circulation falls, so does income, aggregate demand and imports. The gold standard, therefore, still ensures an automatic mechanism which tends to bring the balance of payments into equilibrium, even if this operates via income and employment variations rather than through prices.

According to Keynesian theory, if prices are constant, an increase in the quantity of money in surplus countries lowers interest rates. The fall of interest rates on bank accounts and on bonds causes capital to transfer from surplus to deficit countries, where the reduction in the amount of money in circulation makes interest rates rise. Therefore under the gold standard even capital movements help to achieve balance of payments adjustments.

174

11.6 FLEXIBLE EXCHANGE RATES, THE EFFECTS OF DEVALUATION AND CURRENCY REGULATIONS

The gold standard lasted until the First World War. The attempts to revive it in the post war period failed, as all countries ended by giving up the convertibility of their currencies into gold.

The main reason why governments were persuaded to eliminate convertibility was that deficit countries did not want to accept deflation, that is to reduce the amount of money in circulation in order to make income and consequently imports fall and thus restore balance of payments equilibrium.

Internal deflation, in fact, would have led to unemployment, with negative political and social consequences at a time when governments pursued full employment as their main objective. Monetary policy was used to grant an aggregate demand level that would guarantee full employment, but this often entailed high internal demand (consumption, investments and public expenditure) and consequently low exports[5] together with a high volume of imports,[6] which could not ensure equilibrium in the balance of payments. This indicates a conflict between internal equilibrium (full employment) and external equilibrium (i.e. that of the balance of payments); this will be examined in the coming paragraphs.

When the gold standard was abandoned between the two wars a *flexible*, and in some periods controlled, *exchange rate regime* occurred.

If currencies cannot be converted into gold, their exchange rate is not fixed as in the gold standard, but fluctuates without restriction, depending on currencies demand and supply.

Let us consider a *deficit* country with an excess of imports over exports, for instance Britain. The supply of sterling (with which agents buy foreign currencies to pay for imports) is higher than demand (coming from foreign agents who must pay for British exports). Therefore, sterling's price, that is its exchange rate with respect to other currencies, falls. A devaluation (i.e. depreciation) of the exchange rate[7] makes British goods cheaper for foreigners (even if the prices in sterling are unchanged) as a smaller amount of foreign currency is now needed to buy the same amount of sterling. Therefore, British exports rise.

At the same time the devaluation makes imports more expensive, given that now more sterling is needed to buy the same amount of foreign currency, and British imports therefore fall.

The opposite occurs in *surplus* countries: the exchange rate undergoes a revaluation (i.e. an appreciation), making domestic goods more expensive for foreigners and therefore making exports fall, while imports become less expensive, and therefore rise.

Hence in the gold standard balance of payments equilibrium is achieved by means of variations of prices or, more realistically, of income and employment, while the exchange rate remains fixed.

In a flexible exchange rate system, on the contrary, the equilibrium of balance of payments is achieved by exchange rate variations, while prices and domestic income remain unchanged.

While at first sight it appears that the flexible exchange system avoids the shortcomings of the gold standard, it is immediately evident that this is not the case. As we have seen, a devaluation raises the competitiveness of exports, but makes imports more costly. If an economy is based on the transformation of imported raw materials into manufactures (and this is the case of many industrial countries), it is not possible to reduce imports without creating unemployment in the industrial sector. Moreover, by making imports of raw materials more expensive, a devaluation leads to an increase of domestic prices (cost-push inflation).

Trade unions could react by asking for, and obtaining, wage increases. Social conflicts could thus lead to an inflationary process, determining further price increases, a deficit in the balance of payments and a new devaluation of the exchange rate, worsening the cost-push inflation. This would determine a vicious circle of devaluation, inflation, devaluation, like the one which occurred in various countries (e.g. Britain and Italy) in the Seventies. On the other hand, an appreciation of the exchange rate in surplus countries, by reducing exports, could lead to unemployment in some industrial sectors.

However, it could happen that a devaluation of the exchange rate in a deficit country would not improve the balance of payments. A devaluation ensures a smaller quantity of foreign currency for the same volume of exports and a higher outflow of the (domestic) depreciated currency for the same volume of imports. In order for a devaluation to reduce the difference between outflow and inflow of foreign currency (i.e. the balance of payments' deficit), the volume of exports must rise and/or the volume of imports must fall[8] enough to balance (and overtake) the negative effect we have mentioned.

Many economists have shown that this may not always be the case. In fact, the convenience of buying a product does not derive solely from its price, but also from other elements, like its quality, the fact that it is well-known on markets and, if it is a product that needs upkeep and repair (like cars, television sets and so on), from the existence of a network of repair shops.

All these elements add up to the fact that in the short run a devaluation cannot lead to a large increase in exports. Moreover, as we have seen, a country importing mainly raw materials cannot cut them easily, at least in the short run, without curtailing domestic production and employment.

In the long run, however, firms can follow strategies tailored at penetrating foreign markets and therefore a devaluation can lead to a consistent rise in exports. Similarly, a devaluing country can substitute some imports with domestic goods (for instance, oil with nuclear power, natural fibres with synthetic ones, and so on), reducing imports. Thus a devaluation of the exchange rate rarely improves the balance of payments in the short run, but it can do so in the long run.

The *absorption approach* underlines that a devaluation cannot raise exports if the economy is in full employment. In this case production cannot be raised and the increase of exports can only take place if part of the production consumed internally or, better still, absorbed internally (by consumption, investment or by public sector demand) is used for exports. Therefore, if the economy is in full employment, devaluation will raise exports only if it is adopted together with a restrictive fiscal or monetary policy, reducing domestic absorption, i.e. domestic demand.

Economists of the *New Cambridge School* in England identify the component of absorption to be reduced in public spending financed through a budget deficit. They therefore suggest reducing the budget deficit in order to contain the balance of payments deficit.

According to other authors, a restrictive monetary policy is the best instrument to reduce domestic demand. Naturally this point is controversial. In fact, a restrictive monetary policy may lead to a reduction of income and employment and therefore of demand and production. A country with a balance of payments deficit may want to reduce domestic demand, but not production, otherwise it would risk not being able to increase exports. In any case the reduction in domestic demand should be larger than the reduction in production.

The *monetary approach to the balance of payments* on the other hand maintains that a balance of payments deficit leads *per se* to a reduction of the money supply, unless the central bank creates money in some other way to counteract the effect of this reduction (see chapter four). Such a reduction does not lead to a fall in the price level or in employment; but, given that agents (families and firms) want to keep a fixed amount of liquidity (that is cash and bank deposits), if money supply falls, they do not reduce their demand for cash or deposits, but, in order to keep the same amount of liquidity, they curtail expenditure on consumption and investment, i.e. demand. In this way, the balance of payments deficit automatically falls. This theory follows the approach of those who think that economies are basically stable and that they have in themselves automatic mechanisms to correct disequilibria, which render economic policies useless. However, the monetary approach to the balance of payments has been criticised for its extremely unrealistic assumptions.

One of the main shortcomings of a flexible exchange rate system is the uncertainty it creates among economic agents, who are unable to predict a given amount of foreign currency in domestic money. While agents can reduce risk by operating in forward markets, this is expensive, and in many countries forward markets are not sufficiently developed.

To reduce uncertainty, monetary authorities normally buy and sell monies on currency markets, in order to limit exchange rate fluctuations resulting from market forces. In this case one has a 'managed (or dirty) float', while a 'clean float' takes place when the authorities do not act on currency markets. In practice, a 'clean float' does not exist.

Another controversial point concerns the role of capital movements under a flexible exchange rate system. If speculators expect the exchange rate of a country (for instance Britain) to depreciate and that of another one (Germany) to appreciate, they sell the currency of the former (sterling) and buy that of the latter (marks). This actually makes sterling depreciate and the mark appreciate. If Britain has a balance of payments deficit and Germany a surplus, this helps adjustment.

However, as we have said, exchange rate fluctuations, and in particular abrupt and intense ones, may be very inconvenient. Moreover, speculative capital movements could continue even after the balance of payments has returned to equilibrium, starting to have a destabilising effect.

178

Speculation can, in many cases, have destabilising effects. For instance, at any moment speculators could buy large quantities of marks, causing it to appreciate. This could create expectations for a further revaluation, and would encourage even small operators to buy marks. The process of revaluation would be strengthened and speculators could then sell marks at a higher price.

International cooperation was very intense from 1870 to 1914, when most countries respected the rules of the gold standard. During the inter-war period the currency convertibility was weakened, when each country followed nationalist policies, trying to achieve the exchange rate that would guarantee full employment, even if this ran counter to the interests of other countries or reduced international trade.

Many countries devalued their exchange rates to raise exports, while limiting imports by means of protectionist measures (duties, quotas, etc.) and other types of intervention aimed at modifying currency movements directly. One of these, for instance, was the introduction of a rule whereby importers asking for foreign currency had to get authorisation from the central bank (or the exchange office), who could then select the goods to be imported and, in some cases, refuse or delay the authorisation. The same can be said for other measures of *currency regulation*, such as limiting the amount of money allowed to be taken abroad by tourists and others, limiting or prohibiting capital exports, controlling bank currency operations, adopting compensatory agreements whereby two countries agree generally on a bilateral basis to balance their commercial accounts eliminating or reducing currency movements. In the Thirties the flexible exchange rate system thus became a regime of *regulated exchange rates*.

11.7 THE PURCHASING POWER PARITY THEORY

The exchange rate between two currencies is determined by their demand and supply. However, there are other forces in action too.

In 1922 the Swedish economist *Gustav Cassel* introduced the *purchasing power parity theory* and maintained that *the equilibrium exchange rate between two currencies tends to equate the ratio between their internal purchasing powers*. For instance, if in the United States one dollar buys the same amount of goods that can be bought in Britain for 0.4 pounds, the exchange rate between dollar and sterling is one dollar for 0.4 pounds; thus no one will purchase one dollar for more than 0.4 pounds, given that with 0.4 pounds one can purchase in Britain what could be bought in the United States with one dollar.

If the exchange rate between the two currencies differs from the ratio between their purchasing powers, it will adjust in order to be equal. Assume that a textbook costs one dollar in the United States and 0.7 pounds in Britain and that the exchange rate is of one dollar for 0.5 pounds. A British student does not buy the textbook at home, because it costs 0.7 pounds. Instead, with 0.5 pounds he purchases one dollar, which then allows him to buy the textbook in the United States. This costs him half a pound rather than 0.7. Therefore, if this is the case, the British sell sterling on currency markets and purchase dollars (with which they buy American textbooks). The supply of sterling rises, making its price, i.e. the exchange rate between sterling and the dollar, fall. The process goes on until the exchange rate between sterling and the dollar reaches the level of one dollar for 0.7 sterling, that is the ratio between the purchasing powers of the two currencies.

Every time the internal purchasing power of one of the two currencies changes, even the exchange rate changes, through the mechanism described. If the internal purchasing power of sterling falls (that is, prices in Britain rise),[9] while that of the dollar remains stable (i.e. prices in the United States are unchanged), the exchange rate between sterling and the dollar worsens.

According to Cassel's theory, the exchange rate between two currencies is determined by the level of domestic prices in the two countries and it changes whenever prices (i.e. the currency's purchasing power) change in either country.

Cassel's theory does not contradict the idea that the exchange rate is determined by a currency's demand and supply. In fact, Cassel maintains that the demand and supply for currencies reflect each country's internal purchasing power, as we have seen in the example above. Therefore the equilibrium exchange rate (determined by the demand and supply for currencies) is determined as the ratio between the internal purchasing powers of the two currencies.

Cassel's theory has been criticised from various points of view. For instance, it is unclear which prices should be considered when measuring the internal purchasing power of each currency, if only those of internationally tradable goods or of all goods. This point remains controversial. Moreover, demand and supply for a currency depend not only on its internal purchasing power, but also on other elements. For instance, an agent expecting the exchange rate between sterling and mark to fall, sells sterling to purchase marks. These sales and purchases of currencies, which represent speculative capital movements, albeit changing the exchange rate between sterling and the mark, may have little or no relation with the internal purchasing power of each currency.

Recent experience has shown that speculative capital movements can make exchange rates differ markedly from purchasing power parities. One example is given by the fluctuations of the dollar in the Eighties. Cassel's theory, therefore, appears to be true only in some situations as a first approximation.

NOTES

1. If, for instance, we assume that, by exporting one gallon of wine, Portugal gets 110 pounds from Britain (rather than 119), trade would be even more convenient for Britain. It would still be convenient for Portugal, even if less than in the previous example, given that with 110 pounds it could import more than one yard of cloth from Britain (paying for it more than 90 pounds per yard for it).
   Note moreover, we have assumed the cost of cloth and of wine in Portugal to be equal both to 70 only for the sake of simplicity, given that this makes the difference in the advantage between the two goods immediately evident (70/120; 70/90). The example, however, could be easily proven even with different costs.
2. In bilateralism country A tends to import from country B goods for a value equal to that of the goods it sells to B; A tries to behave like this with respect to every country.
3. The *exchange rate* between currency A and currency B is the amount of the latter necessary to buy one unit of A. For instance, the exchange rate between sterling and the dollar is the amount of dollars necessary to buy one pound.
4. The *balance of payments* registers a country's economic relations with the rest of the world: not only exports and imports of goods (which represent the *trade balance*), but also invisibles (tourism, freight, etc.); unilateral transfers (emigrants' remittances, donations) and capital movements (financial and direct investments).
5. In fact, if an excessively large part of national income is absorbed for internal uses (consumption, investment and public expenditure), only a small part remains for exports.
6. A high level of aggregate demand entails a high level of demand for foreign goods.

7. In current usage, the term 'devaluation' (for instance of sterling) can refer to two different phenomena: devaluation of the exchange rate between sterling, the dollar or any other foreign currency. This is what we are dealing with. Another phenomenon is the loss of sterling's *domestic* purchasing power, which in practice means that, following an increase in domestic prices (inflation), the same amount of sterling can buy fewer goods.

8. A fall of imports obviously determines a reduction of the outflow of foreign currency.

9. A currency's internal purchasing power (i.e. its value) is the reciprocal of the price level.

12 The evolution of the international economic relations after the Second World War

12.1 THE BRETTON WOODS SYSTEM

After the Second World War international economic relations returned to a multilateral system managed by the International Monetary Fund, which was *created in 1944 by the Bretton Woods' agreements*, initially signed by thirty nine countries.[1] Since then almost all countries have accepted the agreements, with the exception of the socialist ones which, having a centralised trading system, remain excluded from these relations, and have their own specific organisations (for instance, the CMEA Bank). In recent years, however, in the wake of political change, many East European countries have asked to join the IMF.

According to the Bretton Woods agreements, each country had to fix the parity of its currency with respect to the dollar and keep the exchange rate within a fluctuation band of 1 percent above or below the parity.[2]

Assume an official parity between dollar and the French franc of one dollar for 4.90 francs. If, due to the action of demand and supply, the exchange rate reached the level of one dollar for 4.85 francs (that is if the franc appreciated by one per cent above the parity), the Bank of France had to sell francs (buying dollars), thus allowing the franc to depreciate and bringing the exchange rate in line with its parity. If the exchange reached one dollar for 4.95 francs, the Bank of France had to do the opposite, buying francs. Therefore, exchange rates were essentially kept

183

fixed by the intervention of central banks in currency markets rather than through the gold standard mechanism.

While every country fixed its currency's parity with respect to the dollar, the latter had its own *parity with respect to gold*. Its reciprocal was *gold's official price*; in 1934 it was fixed by the American Government at thirty five dollars an ounce and it remained unchanged until 1972.

The Bretton Woods system introduced a form of convertibility that was much more limited than the gold standard. Each country was obliged to ensure the *convertibility* of its currency into dollars, at the current exchange rate (i.e. practically, at the official parity), *for non residents*. Consider a country like France. Foreigners or French citizens living abroad could ask the Bank of France to convert francs into dollars. However, French citizens were not granted the same right, even if in many countries the law allowed residents to get some foreign currency, e.g. for tourism, or for paying imported goods.

Besides the convertibility of domestic currencies into dollars, the new system granted also the *convertibility of dollars into gold, limitedly to central banks*. Only these could ask the Government of the United States to convert their dollars into gold. The Bretton Woods system was therefore a *gold exchange standard*.

Exchange rates were practically fixed, but parity changes of domestic currencies with respect to the dollar were allowed. If a country thought that its economy had undergone structural changes and that its parity would no longer ensure the equilibrium of the balance of payments, it could change it. However, once a new parity was fixed, intervention on currency markets had to keep the exchange rate within a fluctuation band of one per cent above or beneath it.[3] The Bretton Woods system was therefore radically different from a flexible exchange rate regime, where currencies would appreciate or depreciate every day, according to demand and supply. If a proposed parity variation was greater than ten per cent, the country in question had to ask for the authorisation of the International Monetary Fund.

The *adjustement of the balance of payments* took place by a process which was close to that of the gold standard. A deficit country having an excess of imports over exports, would pay for this difference by an outflow of dollars. The fall of currency reserves in the deficit country did not automatically entail a reduction of the domestic supply of money, as in the gold standard, because the central bank could create money through the other channels. However, if the deficit – and the outflow of dollars – persisted, no country could afford to undergo an endless loss of reserves. Therefore a restrictive monetary and fiscal policy had to be adopted to reduce income and demand, in order to curtail imports and raise exports. The opposite would happen for a surplus country.

Therefore, the adjustment of balance of payments would occur by means of a variation of income and employment, while the exchange rates would remain practically fixed. A variation of parities, that could take place to correct structural balance of payments disequilibria, remained an exceptional remedy.

12.2 THE EVOLUTION AND THE DECLINE OF THE BRETTON WOODS SYSTEM

In the immediate postwar period, Europe experienced the problem of a *dollar scarcity*. In fact, the dollars donated by the US Government to the European countries via the European Recovery Program (ERP, the so called Marshall Plan) were used by the latter to buy foodstuffs, industrial machinery and equipment from America, which was the only country able to produce such goods. In these years the United States balance of payments had only a very small deficit (essentially due to donations and overseas investments), while its trade account was in surplus, given that exports were much greater than imports.

By the late Fifties, however, the situation started changing. As European and Japanese economies, completely exhausted by the war, started gaining strength and competitiveness on international markets, they imported less from the United States and exported more to the rest of the world, reducing the share of American exports. The United States trade account surplus started falling and the deficit in its balance of payments rose, even due to American investment in Europe and to military spending abroad (the US kept troops in various areas of the world, and imported raw materials for military purposes).

The number of dollars in circulation outside the United States started to increase: moreover, only a small part of them was in central banks safes, given that most were used directly by firms and by commercial banks for trade and for financial transactions, which were growing rapidly, given the strengthening of economic integration between Western countries. The *eurodollar market* started to develop; it consisted of all the dollars that were outside the United States and outside central banks safes.

The continuous growth of the American balance of payments deficit soon led to a situation where the amount of dollars outside the United States was much greater than the quantity of gold which it owned. In the second half of the Sixties the United States could not convert more than one fifth of the amount of dollars in circulation in the world at the existing parity (thirty five dollars for one ounce of gold). European governments thus started increasing their requests to the American Treasury for converting their dollars into gold, given that the United States was the only country which benefited from the privilege of buying goods abroad with its own currency, without having *de facto* to convert it into gold (or in any other form of reserve), and could therefore print an illimited quantity of it.[4]

The Americans, on the contrary, felt that their deficit was due to military expenditures, to which European countries contributed very little (albeit benefiting from the allied defensive system) and to EEC protectionism that restricted United States' agricultural exports to Europe as well as sales of Japanese industrial products, which were directed towards American markets.

In the second half of the Sixties, however, the principle that the creation of international liquidity (i.e. of means of payment to be used for international transactions) should be separated from the United States' deficit on foreign accounts slowly started to be accepted. The amount of dollars available for international transactions depended on the size of the deficit in the United States balance of payments, which, in turn, reflected the country's policies (both monetary and fiscal). For instance, an expansionary aggregate demand policy, by raising prices, would make American exports less competitive and would thus increase its foreign deficit. Monetary and fiscal policies adopted by the United States, however, were tailored to pursue internal objectives (for instance, full employment), while the amount of international liquidity should have grown in line with the volume of world trade. This, however, could be possible only if a new instrument of liquidity, other than the dollar, was created.

Contrary to what some economists thought, gold could not be used to accomplish this task again, even because there is a technical limit to the amount of gold that can be made available, while world trade was growing rapidly.

In 1969 a system of multilateral credits called *special drawing rights* was created under the IMF, according to rules agreed upon by member states. The system, which was managed by the Fund, was intended to give life to an international means of payment, adding up to existing liquidity.

In the same period, as the United States' deficit continued to grow rapidly, a *double market for gold* was created (1968). Until then, the price of gold had been determined by market demand and supply for industrial and other uses. It had remained very close to the official price of gold, due to the intervention of the central banks of the main industrial countries, especially the United States, which sold gold when its price tended to grow beyond the level of thirty five dollars per ounce, and bought it when the opposite occurred.

However, the growing demand for gold depleted American reserves. In 1968 the so called double market for gold was created: together with an official market (for monetary purposes) reserved for central banks, where they pledged to exchange gold at the official price (thirty five dollars per ounce), a free market was introduced for private agents (firms, goldsmiths, commercial banks), where the price would be determined by demand and supply. Central banks, moreover, pledged not to purchase or sell gold on the free market. With this agreement gold ended up to become a 'frozen' i.e. an immovable component of the reserves of central banks.

Since then the price of gold on the free market continued to rise until it touched the level of 190 dollars per ounce between 1974 and 1975. The American foreign deficit grew and inflation rose in almost all countries, reducing the public's reliance on currencies (including the dollar) and encouraging people to buy gold.

The deficit in the American balance of payments and the consequent expansion of the eurodollar market created many problems for European countries as it exposed their economies to *sudden inflows or outflows of dollars, leading respectively to inflation or deflation.*

Let us assume that the owners of eurodollars decide to buy a large amount of German bonds, given that they represent a safe and profitable investment. Therefore agents buy marks giving (i.e. selling) dollars. The demand for marks on currency markets grows and the exchange rate between the mark and the dollar increases. When it reaches one per cent above the parity, the German central bank must sell marks (to prevent a further revaluation), i.e. purchase dollars. By selling large amounts of marks, however, it raises the money in circulation, and thus creates inflation.

These problems are strongly reduced by the adoption of a flexible exchange rate system. In fact, when the demand for marks increases, if the German central bank does not intervene selling marks, the amount of money in circulation does not increase and therefore there is no inflation. However, if this is the case, the exchange rate between the mark and the dollar appreciates and the system becomes one of flexible exchange rates. On the other hand, an appreciation of the mark, by making it more expensive, gradually reduces its demand.

To avoid these problems, since the late Sixties central banks have limited their intervention on currency markets and have left exchange rates fluctuate with respect to the dollar beyond the limit envisaged by the Bretton Woods agreements (one per cent above and beneath the parity). *In this way, the world economy passed from a fixed exchange rates regime to a flexible one.*

Moreover, there was another reason causing the international monetary system to switch to flexible exchange rates. Since the early Seventies the prices of commodities started growing at very different rates across industrial countries; according to the theory of the purchasing power parity, the exchange rates of their currencies could not remain fixed.

For instance, in Britain strong trade unions led to high wage rises and hence to inflation. Therefore, the prices of British products rose faster than those of German ones. Consequently, so long as the exchange rate between the mark and sterling remained unchanged, British exports became more expensive, and therefore fell. This, in turn, curtailed the demand for sterling on currency markets (on behalf of foreign purchasers of British goods), and therefore led to a devaluation of sterling's exchange rate. To contrast this tendency, the Bank of England should have bought sterling, but, to do so, it had to offer dollars. As the process of depreciation of sterling's exchange rate went on, the Bank of England did not have enough dollars (i.e. reserves) to stop sterling's depreciation and to keep it within the limits envisaged by the Bretton Woods agreements.

Therefore, for these reasons (strong speculative capital movements, differences in inflation rates), *starting in the early Seventies, the world switched from a regime of fixed exchange rates to one of flexible rates*: one of the main features of the Bretton Woods system collapsed.

In August 1971 the President of the United States Richard Nixon announced the inconvertibility of the dollar. Central banks could no longer take their dollars to the United States' Treasury asking to convert them into gold. Thus, the other main aspect of the Bretton Woods system collapsed, although Nixon's decision really sanctioned something that already had occurred in practice, given that the amount of dollars outside the United States was enormously greater than the American gold reserves (valued at thirty five dollars per ounce). Later on, Nixon twice devalued the dollar's parity with respect to gold, bringing its reciprocal – the official price of gold – from thirty five to some fourty two dollars per ounce. However, this did not bear a great significance, given that the dollar was (and still is) inconvertible into gold. Even at the new parity the United States could not convert all the dollars in circulation in the world.

European governments maintained that, given the dollar's inconvertibility into gold, an official parity between the dollar and gold (and hence an official price of gold) had no practical significance. They now wanted the United States to abolish the official gold market, in order to let central banks sell gold on the free market, where its price would be determined by demand and supply, and would therefore be much higher than the official price. As we have said, the price of gold on the free market had reached 190 dollars per ounce.

Actually, since 1973, member countries of the International Monetary Fund had started moving in this direction, *deciding, in the Jamaica meeting of January 1976, to abolish the official price of gold, and hence the double market for gold.* The agreement, moreover, authorised the International Monetary Fund to give part of its gold back to the countries that had deposited it as a membership quota, and to sell another part of it, using the revenue in favour of developing countries. In this way, gold lost its role as the basis of the international monetary system, and became a commodity like any other. In 1979 the price of gold went beyond 600 dollars per ounce.

Given the abolition of the convertibility of the dollar into gold, the present system of monetary international relations cannot be called a gold exchange standard any more, but has become a *dollar standard*, in which payments for international commercial and financial transactions are settled in dollars, that are inconvertible.

On the other hand, notwithstanding the dollar's inconvertibility, economic agents continue to use it in international trade and in financial transactions, because it is the currency they believe is most reliable. In fact, if an individual (resident outside the United States) remains with some dollars, he can always buy the commodities produced in the United States. On the other hand, what could he do with the currency of a small and underdeveloped state, that produces almost nothing?

Therefore, in the early Seventies, the Bretton Woods system came to an end. All the attempts to revive a system of fixed rates, or a managed float, have failed. The fact that each country lets its currency fluctuate with respect to the others does not prevent central banks from intervening on the exchange rates market to reduce fluctuations. The present regime, in other words, is one of a 'dirty float'.

12.3 THE RECENT EVOLUTION OF INTERNATIONAL MONETARY RELATIONS

The *energy (or oil) crisis* contributed in raising the instability of international monetary relations. In 1973, oil producing countries, having reached a monopolistic agreement, decided to greatly increase oil prices, in an attempt to obtain more manufactures for a given amount of oil. Industrial countries were hit by this, and had large deficits in their balances of payments.

Their governments were thus obliged to adopt restrictive fiscal and monetary policies, which, in turn, by reducing investment and employment, reduced the demand for oil, and limited its price rise. By means of the policies that restricted domestic demand and stepped up productivity, industrial countries managed to raise their exports, importing oil at its new prices, paying, that is, the so called *oil bill.* At the same time, technological innovations and substitution with other forms of energy allowed to reduce oil consumption.

Shortly after, however, a different adjustment mechanism came into action. In order to buy the same amount of oil at the new prices, the United States undertook an expansionary monetary policy, continuously putting dollars into the international monetary system through the deficit in its balance of payments. Moreover, the oil producing countries deposited the largest part of their soaring dollar revenues (due to the oil price rises) in Western banks, which made the eurodollar market expand greatly. This market, in turn, redirected the eurodollars in the form of loans to industrial countries, which thus financed their balance of payments' deficits.

The rise in the dollar supply determined inflation in the United States and, in general, an increase in the (dollar) prices of manufactures. In only four years the terms of trade between manufactures and oil products (i.e. the ratio of their prices) gradually returned to the pre-1973 situation. This showed that *the monopoly of the production of dollars* (which belongs to the United States) *is more important than the monopoly of the production of oil*, which then belonged to OPEC.

While manufactures and oil prices grew at grossly the same rate, the prices of other raw materials remained relatively stable, leading to a growing impoverishment of non-oil producing developing countries. The effect of this redistribution of real income among countries is well known.

In a situation in which the United States endorsed an expansionary monetary policy and the dollar was weak on international currency markets, other industrial countries could, within certain limits, follow an independent policy for the exchange rate between their currencies and the dollar. The two extreme cases of industrial countries' economic policies are Germany and Italy. Western Germany opposed inflationary pressures coming from the dollar area by adopting a restrictive monetary policy, which determined an appreciation of the mark-dollar exchange rate. Italy, on the contrary, absorbed the inflationary pressures due to the American monetary policy and pegged the lira to the dollar.

Starting in 1978, oil producing countries raised oil prices again and tried to introduce an indexing mechanism to avoid repeating the 1973-77 situation. The oil price was thus pegged to the price of manufactures or to the growth rate of income in industrial countries.

The second wave of oil price rises, however, soon came to an end, due to the different economic policy adopted by the United States. The Reagan Administration pursued three objectives of domestic economic policy: the reduction of public expenditure, detaxation, deregulation, i.e. a reduction of the government's regulation of private activities. These measures were intended to stimulate private investment, the growth of production and, at the same time, to reduce inflation. The reduction of

191

public expenditure would have to ensure an increase in private investment without determining inflationary pressures or tension in interest rates. The reduction of taxes and deregulation would help raise the incentives for private investment and economic activity. These were the main targets of the *supply side economics*, or *Reaganomics*, according to which a rise in income could not stem from a policy of demand expansion, which would have led only to inflation and a soaring foreign debt, but should derive from a rise in the economy's productive capacity.

As it is well known, however, by raising military expenditure without lowering social expenditure sufficiently, the Reagan Administration did not manage to reduce public expenditure. Moreover, deregulation failed to produce significant effects on investment. All these factors, added to the reduction in taxes, determined a strong expansion of the public deficit.

American authorities, however, refused to finance the deficit by expanding money supply. In other words, they supported the principle of the separation (i.e. divorce) between the Treasury and the Fed[5] and pursued a restrictive monetary policy in order to reduce the rate of inflation. This, in turn, determined a strong rise in interest rates, that reached exceptionally high levels. High interest rates had essentially three types of effect.

Within the United States they had a restrictive effect, determining an initial fall in investment. However, this ceased soon. After the deep recession of 1980-82, starting from 1983 the American economy underwent an exceptional boom, determined both by confidence in the new political course and by the expansionary budget policy adopted by the Reagan Administration.

Outside the United States, high interest rates coupled with the fall of inflation, both current and expected, made real interest rates soar. This effect spread rapidly to the eurodollar market, determining a huge increase of the demand for financial assets denominated in dollars and, consequently, a strong appreciation of the dollar on currency markets.

Moreover, the rise of interest rates on the eurodollar market determined an exceptional rise in the financial burden of heavily indebted countries, like developing ones and some centrally planned economies (Poland, Hungary, East Germany and Yugoslavia). The negative effect of the rise of interest rates added to the appreciation of the dollar, in which most of the debts of developing countries are denominated. By the mid-

Eighties many less developed countries were on the verge of economic collapse. However, such a danger was later averted, at least temporarily, thanks to the action of a number of large banks, international institutions and of the United States' Government. In such a situation, the actual independence of countries other than the United States is very limited.

In fact, whilst the dollar is weak (as in the Seventies), industrial countries can choose between the German and the Italian option. On the contrary, when the dollar is strong (and its strength is due to financial factors, that make it requested as a means of international investment, as during most of the Eighties), the authorities of the other industrial countries, given their size and the limited diffusion of their currencies, do not have the possibility of pursuing an autonomous exchange rate policy *vis à vis* the dollar.

The events of the Eighties have shown that, by adopting purely financial measures, the United States is able to determine a strong appreciation of the dollar, i.e. to raise its purchasing power. Moreover, experience has proved that a high dollar can coexist even for a long period with a high deficit of the American current account. All this shows that there has been a transfer of real resources towards the United States.

The high exchange rate of the dollar with respect to the currencies of the other industrial countries reduced American exports and raised imports, leading to a high deficit of the United States balance of trade.

On the other hand, Germany and Japan had high exports and large surpluses in their trade balances. Foreign investors, however, and essentially German and Japanese ones, bought big amounts of American securities (Treasury bills, bonds, equities, etc.), ensuring an inflow of capital to the United States that compensated the balance of trade deficit.

The dollar's depreciation in the second half of the Eighties was not able to reduce the trade deficit of the United States adequately, and this could have been expected, due to the general considerations mentioned in paragraph 11.6.

Presently,the situation is characterised by strong disequilibria in the balances of payments and by the presence of large amounts (i.e. stocks) of monetary and financial assets that move from one country to another. The behaviour of these stocks is always largely determined by the economic policy of the United States which, by varying interest rates, produces immediate effects on these stocks, which tend to move towards those countries which offer higher revenues on financial assets.

Disequilibrium tends to persist and, even if it has determined some financial crises such as October 1987, so far it has not created major problems for the real economy. In October 1987 a lack of confidence on firms' profitability spread among agents who, believing that many firms were in trouble, sold their shares, determining a fall of their prices. Due to agents' increasing lack of confidence, the sudden fall of quotations on the New York stock exchange spread to world financial markets. However, contrary to what happened in 1929, the crisis did not spread to the economy's real variables. In 1929, after the stock exchange collapse, there was a fall in the demand for consumption and investment goods and therefore a fall of prices, employment, wages and GNP. Nothing similar took place in 1987; on the contrary, the Unites States' GNP continued to grow at a high rate.

Even international trade continued to grow, different from what happened in the Thirties. Moreover, even if both the convertibility of the dollar into gold and fixed exchange rates have ceased, one main point of the Bretton Woods system is still in force, i.e. the convertibility of national currencies into dollars for non residents. For instance, someone owning marks, sterling or liras (and not being a resident of Germany, Britain or Italy) can have these currencies converted into dollars by the central banks of these countries. This possibility makes the present situation completely different from that of the Thirties, even if sometimes there is a certain tendency towards protectionism.

At present, in a situation characterised by flexible exchange rates and strong balance of payments disequilibria there is an area of exchange rate stability, represented by the member countries of the *European Monetary System* (EMS), that started in 1979 and created an exchange system among EEC currencies fluctuating within fairly large and predetermined limits. The central element of the EMS is the ECU (which in French means shield, and corresponds to the initials of european currency unit). The ECU is a fictitious currency. It has a *conversion rate* (i.e. and exchange rate) with each national currency, which represents its *central rate*, or *course*. For each currency the conversion rate was fixed by an agreement undertaken by the Governments of the European Community countries upon entering the EMS and can be modified only by a new agreement among the Governments. Since 1979 there have been various modifications of the central rates.

Given that each currency has a central rate with the ECU, these determine immediately the *bilateral parities* between currencies. For instance, if one ECU is equal respectively to 1.4 sterling and to two marks, two marks will be equal to 1.4 sterling and hence one mark is equal to 0.7 sterling. Each country can let its exchange rate fluctuate with respect to the other currencies by 2.25 percent above and below the central rate. Central banks must intervene to buy or sell their currency every time it appreciates or depreciates beyond these limits. Naturally the EMS may last while the divergences between the inflation rates of member countries are not too great. In fact, whenever large and persistent divergences occur, exchange rates' fluctuations can get out of control, as in the Seventies.

This system mainly concerns industrial countries with market economies. On the contrary, most underdeveloped countries control, often very tightly, foreign economic relations, and consequently exchange rates. These countries often resort to *multiple exchange rates*, on the basis of which the central bank fixes different prices for foreign currencies according to buyers' different uses. For instance, currency may be sold at a very high price to buyers using it to go abroad for tourism or to import luxury goods. On the other hand, it can be sold at a lower price to buyers who import industrial machinery, that is important for the country's development.

Even Socialist countries are outside the system of international relations under the International Monetary Fund. These countries pursue bilateralism of trade both with market economies and between themselves. As already mentioned, bilateralism consists in a country keeping its balance of payments with each other country in equilibrium. Given that this system represents an obstacle to the development of trade, it is viable only when commerce is scarce. In Socialist countries foreign trade is under the state monopoly, and currencies are not convertible.

In the postwar period, the Soviet Union and East European countries (with the exception of Yugoslavia) created the *CMEA*, that was meant to be the economic union among member countries. In practice, however, CMEA largely missed its target, because East European countries, fearing Soviet hegemony both from the political and the economic point of view, did not want to integrate, or even to coordinate national plans.

Within the CMEA capital movements between one country and another are rare, and are based on bilateral agreements: equally rare is the movement of workers across the borders. Even the exchange of commodities is largely based on bilateralism. Since 1964 a system for multilateral payments was organised and was managed by the CMEA bank, but so far it has had a rather limited development.

The deep and radical changes presently underway in these countries do not allow us to foresee the evolution of their economic and monetary relations in the near future.

12.4 FIXED AND FLEXIBLE EXCHANGE RATES: THEORETICAL ASPECTS AND PRACTICAL EXPERIENCE. THE INTERDEPENDENCE OF THE WORLD ECONOMY

In recent years, the evolution of international monetary relations stimulated a debate among economists on whether a regime of fixed exchange rates is preferable to one of floating exchange rates.

As we have seen, the main argument in favour of fixed rates is that fluctuating exchange rates determine uncertainty among agents and therefore limit trade and international investment. The supporters of floating exchange rates, on the contrary, maintain that flexibility represents an additional instrument with which the authorities can pursue their economic goals, i.e. full employment and balance of payments equilibrium.

Traditionally, it has been maintained that the manipulation of the exchange rate should be targeted to external equilibrium, given that a devaluation allows a reduction in a balance of payments deficit and a revaluation reduces a surplus. As we have seen, however, a devaluation of the exchange rate does not always reduce the foreign trade deficit.

In the debate about the effects of exchange rate variations, one aspect that has often been ignored concerns the consequences on income distribution. A devaluation of sterling, for instance, generates inflation in Britain because it causes both an increase in the prices of imported consumption goods and of raw materials. The latter, in turn, induces firms to raise the prices of finished products. As usual, inflation mainly hurts the social groups with fixed incomes, and especially workers who do not benefit from wage indexation. Such inflationary effects may even determine a reaction in the social groups that have been hit, leading to conflicts and to social problems as those analysed in chapter six.

On the basis of these considerations one may note that, as history shows, flexible exchange rates were not chosen by governments but were a necessity for those countries which were unable to control the rate of domestic inflation. During the period from 1870 to the First World War, when one economy (the British one) was dominant and international relations took place in an 'orderly' fashion, the gold standard, i.e. a fixed rate system, prevailed. In those years industrial countries had high rates of growth and stable, or even declining, prices. Therefore, once a country fixed its currency's parity with respect to gold (and, consequently, its exchange rate), which assured the equilibrium of its balance of payments, this parity could remain unaltered. High growth rates and stable prices were essentially achieved by controlling the social and political framework. In case of a deficit, the adjustment of the balance of payments took place mainly through domestic deflation (fall in income and employment) in the weak countries, while Britain and the other strong countries could correct a deficit by raising interest rates on Treasury bills or other securities and thus attracting foreign capitals. Many agents were in fact willing to invest in Britain, granting it loans when its balance of payments was in deficit, given that they thought that the country and its empire would have always paid back its debts.

In the interwar period Britain was no longer the dominant economy and the United States had not yet achieved enough prestige and influence to substitute Britain. 'Orderly' economic relations broke down as protectionist and autarchic tendencies developed, given that countries preferred not to reduce their external deficits by domestic deflation. In this period there was a system of flexible and then regulated exchange rates.

The Bretton Woods system operated in a way similar to the gold standard. In the postwar period the dominant economy was the American one. Once the European and the Japanese economies recovered, the system worked as a fixed exchange rate one. This continued until the late Sixties without exceptions for those countries that had satisfactory growth rates and stable prices (like Italy), while countries with high inflation rates and consequent balance of payments' deficits (for instance, France and Britain) were obliged to devalue the exchange rate in order to avoid domestic deflation.

The Bretton Woods system collapsed when European countries refused to finance world trade and growth by means of the United States' foreign deficit. As already mentioned, the uncontrolled expansion of the eurodollar market, due to the growing interdependence between Western countries, exposed European economies to sudden inflows and outflows of dollars, with inflationary and deflationary consequences. This fact, together with the growing difficulties met by some countries to keep their price rises in line with those of other countries competing for international markets forced them to allow their exchange rates to float. In this sense, a good example is given by Italy and Britain, where for many years inflation rates were consistently higher than those of other Western countries, on account of particularly intense social conflicts. On more than one occasion both these countries were caught in the vicious circle of inflation and devaluation which we have already described.

One of the main characteristics of the present international economic situation is the *interdependence* between countries, which has consistently grown since the end of the Second World War. Single countries, like the United States, or groups of countries, like the oil producers, transmit impulses to other economic areas, influencing both the world economy and the structure of markets and economies. Obviously, a first impulse generates some consequences, which in turn have others consequences, and produce feedback to the centre. Trasmission mechanisms may be both real (for instance, an increase or a fall in raw materials' prices, or in those of manufactures, an increase or a reduction in exports and in imports) and financial (the effects of interest rates and of exchange rates on capital movements).

Experience shows that the evolution of the American economy still has a very strong influence on the world economy. When the United States pursues an expansionary policy of aggregate demand, the world economy undergoes a boom; this, through an increase in the prices of raw materials, favours growth in developing countries. If the expansion is not carefully controlled, it leads to inflation, that in turn makes the United States' authorities adopt restrictive policies. This determines a world recession, with a negative impact on production and employment in other countries.

In recent years the expansion of the American economy has determined an increase in the demand for raw materials and in their prices, albeit lower than in analogous growth periods in the past. This phenomenon is said to derive from the substitution of raw materials with synthetic ones, that becomes more and more intense with the development of scientific and technological research in industrialised countries, and especially in the United States.

In general, analyses on this subject remain within a Keynesian framework, that focuses only on the effects of the US economic policy on income and employment in the rest of the world. In practice, however, the United States' economic policy influences the world inflation rate and the terms of trade between manufactures and raw materials and hence the distribution of world income among the countries.

This conclusion is confirmed once the role of the United States' monetary policy is considered. By controlling the supply of dollars, the United States can influence, even through the effects on interest and exchange rates, both the level of world economic activity and the distribution of income between different international areas. Recent experience shows that variations of domestic interest rates in the United States produce similar variations in the interest rates on the eurodollar market.

The main reasons that account for the effects of American economic policy on the rest of the world are the size of United States' economy in a framework of interdependence between world economic areas and the role of the dollar on international financial markets.

The experience of the Eighties shows that, whenever it wants, the United States still has an uncontrasted leadership in the world economy. The international monetary system remains therefore monocentric, in the sense that the position of the dollar in international liquidity, and especially in official liquidity of industrial countries, is totally dominant. The same can be said for commercial flows and the real economy. In fact, while it is true that the weight of the United States in world commerce, excluding intra EEC trade, has progressively decreased and that the group of industrial countries with the largest share in international trade is the European Economic Community, it is equally true that, notwithstanding the European Monetary System, the EEC has not got its *own* economic policy, except for limited sectors. No EEC member, not even Germany, can determine the exchange rate policy of its currency with respect to the dollar when the latter is appreciating on the money markets.

Considering what has happend in the postwar period, one can conclude that the effects of the American economic policy are still extremely relevant, both in a regime of fixed exchange rates and of flexible rates. It is interesting to note that in the Sixties, when the Bretton Woods system was still functioning, many economists thought that a system of flexible exchange rates could have isolated the economies of small countries from the effects of American economic policy and from speculative movements of capital. However, the events of the Seventies and Eighties showed that this is not the case. Small countries are always price takers, while the United States can largely influence international prices. Even if it has lost its strength in international trade, the United States remains a price maker, given that it can influence the exchange rate of the dollar, i.e. of the currency in which the imports of the other countries are denominated. Moreover the United States is a price maker on the international financial markets, which are becoming more and more integrated with national markets.

Given the growing interdependence among the economies of the countries, many economists think that international coordination between fiscal and monetary policies could reduce the present balance of payments disequilibria. Surplus countries like Germany and Japan should pursue expansionary policies, while deficit countries, like the United States, should adopt restrictive policies. Naturally, the analysis could be further complicated by considering an appropriate mix of monetary and fiscal policies. Coordination is difficult whenever each country tailors its policies solely to domestic needs. For instance, the United States finds it difficult to curtail the federal deficit, given that it should reduce its military or social expenditure or raise taxes.

Many economists, by using various complex mathematical tools (like game theory) have constructed models that examine the effects of conflicting behaviour patterns versus cooperative ones for the use of monetary and fiscal policies among different countries, reaching general results that are undoubtedly interesting from a theoretical point of view.

NOTES

1. The name derives from the place in the United States where the representatives of the countries who fought against Germany and Japan met.
2. A country would fix its parity at the level that could guarantee the equilibrium of its balance of payments: one can therefore expect the volume of a country's exports to be, in general, equal to that of imports. An excessively high parity (and therefore an excessively high exchange rate) curtails exports and raises

200

imports, giving rise to a balance of payments deficit. An excessively low parity has the opposite effect.

3. For instance, if a country's prices rose more rapidly than those of other countries competing with it on international markets, its exports would fall. A devaluation of the parity would therefore be necessary to bring its balance of payments back to equilibrium.

4. Such a privilege is called *seigniorage right*.

5. The Federal Reserve is the central bank of the United States. Its structure differs from that of the central banks of European countries, but its main functions are the same.

Bibliography

Chapter 1 – NEOCLASSICAL MICROECONOMICS

Gravelle, H.S.E. and Rees, R., *Microeconomics*, Longman, London, 1981.
Layard, P.R.G. and Walters, A.A., *Microeconomic Theory*, MacGraw-Hill, New York, 1978.
Lipsey, R.G., *An Introduction to Positive Economics*, Weidenfeld and Nicolson, London, 1966.
Mansfield, E., *Microeconomics: Theory and Applications*, W.W. Norton and Company, New York, 1975.
Varian, H.R., *Intermediate Microeconomics*, W.W. Norton and Company, New York, 1987.

Chapter 2 – KEYNES

Ackley, G., *Macroeconomic Theory*, MacMillan, New York, 1961.
Hansen, A.H., *A Guide to Keynes*, McGraw-Hill, New York, 1953.
Hillard, J. (ed.), *J.M. Keynes in Retrospect*, Edward Elgar, Aldershot, 1988.
Keynes, J.M., *The General Theory of Employment, Interest and Money*, MacMillan, London, 1936, 1973.
Keynes, M. (ed.), *Essays on John Maynard Keynes*, Cambridge University Press, Cambridge, 1975.
Moggdridge, D.E., *Keynes*, MacMillan, London, 1980.
Thirwall, A.P., *Keynes as a Policy Adviser*, MacMillan, London, 1982.
Vicarelli, F. (ed.), *Keynes' Relevance Today*, MacMillan, London, 1983.

Chapter 3 – THE DEBATE ON THE ROLE OF MONEY: THE THEORY OF THE DEMAND FOR MONEY

Ackley, G., *Macroeconomic Theory*, MacMillan, New York, 1961.

Baumol, W.J., *Portfolio Theory: the Selection of Asset Combinations*, McCaleb-Seiler Publishing Co., New York, 1970.

Coghlan, R., *The Theory of Money and Finance*, MacMillan, London, 1980.

Davidson, P., *Money and the Real World*, MacMillan, London, 1978.

Fisher, D., *Monetary Theory and the Demand for Money*, Martin Robertson, London, 1978.

Friedman, M. (ed.), *Studies in the Quantity Theory of Money*, University of Chicago Press, Chicago, 1956.

Gowland, D., *Money, Inflation and Unemployment*, Harvester Wheatsheaf, Brighton, 1985.

Harris, L., *Monetary Theory*, McGraw-Hill, New York, 1981.

Laidler, D., *The Demand for Money: Theories and Evidence*, Harper and Row, New York, 1977.

Chapter 4 – THE ROLE AND THE EFFECTS OF MONETARY POLICY

Chrystal, K.A., *Controversies in Macroeconomics*, Philip Allan, New York, 1983.

Cuthberson, K., *Macroeconomic Policy. The New Cambridge, Keynesian and Monetarist Controversies*, MacMillan, London, 1979.

Dowd, K., *The State and the Monetary System*, Philip Allan, New York, 1989.

Gowland, D., *Controlling the Money Supply*, Croom Helm, London, 1982.

Greenaway, D., *Current Issues in Macroeconomics*, MacMillan, London, 1989.

Levacic, R. and Rebmann, A., *Macroeconomics. An Introduction to Keynesian-Neoclassical Controversies*, MacMillan, London, 1989.

Chapter 5 – FISCAL AND MONETARY POLICIES AND ECONOMIC STABILITY

Barr, N., *The Economics of the Welfare State*, Weidenfeld and Nicolson, London, 1987.

Frank, J., *The New-Keynesian Economics*, Harvester Wheatsheaf, Brighton, 1986.

Stevenson, A. – Muscatelli, V. – Gregory, M., *Macroeconomic Theory and Stabilisation Policy*, Philip Allan, Oxford, 1988.

Chapter 6 – INFLATION

Bruno, M. and Sachs, J., *Economics of Worldwide Stagflation*, Harvard University Press, Cambridge (Massachussetts), 1985.

Cagan, P., *Persistent Inflation. Historical and Policy Essays*, Columbia University Press, New York, 1979.

Corden, W.M., *Inflation, Exchange Rates and the World Economy. Lectures on International Monetary Economics*, Clarendon Press, Oxford, 1981.

Fallick,J.L., and Elliott, R.F. (eds.), *Incomes Policies, Inflation and Relative Pay*, Allen and Unwin, London, 1981.

Frisch, H., *Theories of Inflation*, Cambridge University Press, Cambridge, 1983.

Hahn, F., *Money and Inflation*, Basil Blackwell, Oxford, 1982.

Jackman, R., Mulvey, C., and Trevithick, J., *The Economics of Inflation*, Martin Robertson, Oxford, 1981.

Mitchell, D.J.B., *Unions, Wages and Inflation*, Brookings Institution, Washington, 1980.

Siven, C.H., *A Study in the Theory of Inflation and Unemployment*, North-Holland, Amsterdam, 1979.

Chapter 7 – CYCLES, GROWTH AND DEVELOPMENT

Barro, R. (ed.), *Modern Business Cycle Theory*, Basil Blackwell, Oxford, 1989.

Branson, W.H., *Macroeconomic Theory and Policy*, Harper and Row, New York, 1979.

Chaudhuri, P., *Economic Theory of Growth*, Harvester Wheatsheaf, New York, 1989.

Freeman, C., Clark, J. and Soete, L., *Unemployment and Technical Innovation: a Study of Long Waves and Economic Development*, F. Pinter, London, 1982.

Gemmell, N., *Structural Change and Economic Development: the Role of the Service Sector*, MacMillan, London, 1986.

Greenway, D., *Economic Development and International Trade*, MacMillan, London, 1988.

Hacche, G., *The Theory of Economic Growth. An Introduction*, MacMillan, London, 1979.

Klein, B.H., *Prices, Wages and Business Cycle. A Dynamic Theory*, Pergamon Press, New York, 1984.

Lucas, R., *Studies in Business-Cycle Theory*, Basil Blackwell, Oxford, 1981.

Mishan, E.J., *The Economic Growth Debate. An Assessment*, Allen and Unwin, Guildford, 1977.

Mullineux, A.W., *The Business Cycle after Keynes: a Contemporary Analysis*, Barnes and Noble Books, Totowa, 1984.

Sorkin, A.L., *Monetary and Fiscal Policy and Business Cycles in the Modern Era*, Lexington, New York, 1988.

Sylos-Labini, P., *The Forces of Economic Growth and Decline*, MIT Press, Cambridge (Massachusetts), 1984.

Chapter 8 – THE PROBLEMS OF UNDERDEVELOPMENT

Agarwala, A.N. and Singh, S.P., *The Economics of Underdevelopment*, Oxford University Press, Oxford, 1963.

Hirschman, A.O.,*The Strategy of Economic Development*, Yale University Press, New Haven, 1969.

Lewis, W.A., *Theory of Economic Growth*, Allen and Unwin, London, 1963.

Myint, H., *Economic Theory and Under-developed Countries*, Duckworth, London, 1957.

Myrdal, G., *The Economics of Developing Countries*, Hutchinson (5th edition), London, 1980.

Nurkse, R., *Problems of Capital Formation in Underdeveloped Countries*, Basil Blackwell, Oxford, 1953.

Nurkse, R., *Patterns of Trade and Development*, Basil Blackwell, Oxford, 1962.

Chapter 9 – WELFARE ECONOMICS, THE THEORY OF ECONOMIC POLICY, ECONOMETRIC ANALYSIS AND EXPERIMENTAL ECONOMICS, THE PROBLEMS OF CENTRALLY PLANNED ECONOMIES

Barrat-Brown, M., *Models in Political Economy: a Guide to the Arguments*, Penguin, Harmondsworth, 1984.

Baumol, W.J., *Economic Theory and Operations Analysis* (4th edition), Prentice Hall, Englewood Cliffs, 1977.

Bornstein, M., *Plan and Market: Economic Reform in Eastern Europe*, Yale University Press, New Haven, 1973.

Caffé, F., *Lezioni di politica economica*, Boringhieri, Torino, 1984.

Charemza, W. and Gronicki, M., *Plans and Disequilibria in Centrally Planned Economies*, North-Holland, Amsterdam, 1988.

Goldberger, A.S., *Econometric Theory*, Wiley, New York, 1984.

Katz, D.A., *Econometric Theory and Applications*, Prentice Hall, Englewood Cliffs, 1982.

Hamilton, F.E., *The Planned Economies*, MacMillan, London, 1979.

Mishan, E.J., *Economic Efficiency and Social Welfare: Selected Essays on Fundamental Aspects of the Economic Theory of Social Welfare*, Allen and Unwin, London, 1981.

Mishan, E.J., *Cost-Benefit Analysis: an Informal Introduction* (4th edition), Unwin Hyman, London, 1988.

Palmerio, G.,*Allocazione efficiente delle risorse e teoria del risparmio ottimale*, Giuffre', Milano, 1967.

Phelps, E., *Economic Justice: Selected Readings*, Penguin, Harmondsworth, 1973.

Pigou, A.C., *The Economics of Welfare*, (4th ed.), AMS Press, New York, 1978.

Sen, A., *Choice, Welfare and Measurement*, Basil Blackwell, Oxford, 1982.

Smith, V.L., *Essays in Experimental Economics*, Cambridge University Press, Cambridge, 1989.

Whiteley, P. (ed.), *Models of Political Economy*, Sage Publications, London, 1980.

Wilczynsky, J.,*The Economics of Socialism: Principles Governing the Operation of the Centrally Planned Economies under the New System*, Allen and Unwin, London, 1982.

Chapter 10 – THE THEORY OF VALUE AND DISTRIBUTION

Bliss, C.J., *Capital Theory and the Distribution of Income*, North-Holland, Amsterdam, 1975.

Dougherty, C., *Interest and Profit*, Meuthen, London, 1980.

Eatwell, J. and Milgate, M. (eds.), *Keynes' Economics and the Theory of Value and Distribution*, Duckworth, London, 1983.

Howard, M., *Modern Theories of Income Distribution*, MacMillan, London, 1979.

Howard, M., *Profits in Economic Theory*, MacMillan, London, 1983.

Mainwaring, L., *Value and Distribution in Capitalist Economies: An Introduction to Sraffian Economics*, Cambridge University Press, Cambridge, 1984.

Milgate, M., *Capital and Employment*, Academic Press, London, 1984.

Morishima, M. and Catephores, G., *Value, Exploitation and Growth*, McGraw-Hill, London, 1978.

Panico, C., *Interest and Profit in the Theories of Value and Distribution*, MacMillan, London, 1988.

Pasinetti, L.L., *Lectures on the Theory of Production*, MacMillan, London, 1977.

Robinson, J., *Collected Economic Papers*, Basil Blackwell, Oxford, 1979.

Chapter 11 – INTERNATIONAL ECONOMIC RELATIONS

Dixit, A. and Norman, V., *Theory of International Trade*, Cambridge University Press, Cambridge, 1980.

Jones, R. and Kenen, P. (eds.), *Handbook of International Economics*, 2 vols., North-Holland, Amsterdam, 1985.

Kenen, P., *The International Economy*, Prentice Hall, Englewood Cliffs, 1989.

Krugman, P. (ed.), *Strategic Trade Policy and the New International Economics*, The MIT Press, Cambridge (Massachusetts), 1988.

Niehans, J., *International Monetary Economics*, Johns Hopkins University Press, Baltimore, 1984.

Saint Phalle, T., *Trade, Inflation and the Dollar*, Oxford University Press, Oxford, 1981.

Salvatore, D., *International Economics*, MacMillan, New York, 1987.

Chapter 12 – THE EVOLUTION OF THE INTERNATIONAL ECONOMIC RELATIONS AFTER THE SECOND WORLD WAR

Greenaway, D., *International Trade Policy: from Tariffs to the New Protectionism*, MacMillan, London, 1983.

Kaldor, N., *Further Essays in Applied Economics*, Duckworth, London, 1978.

Kindleberger, C., *The International Economic Order: Essays in Financial Crisis and International Public Goods*, Harvester Wheatsheaf, New York, 1988.

Kregel, J.A. (ed.), *Distribution, Effective Demand and International Economic Relations*, MacMillan, London, 1983.

Kreinin, M., *International Economics. A Policy Approach*, Harcourt, New York, 1979.

Macbean, A. and Snowden, P., *International Institutions in Trade and Finance*, Allen and Unwin, London, 1981.

Shonfield, A., *International Economic Relations: the Western System in the 1960s and 1970s*, Sage Publications, Beverly Hills, 1976.

Author index

Subject index

212